T0312309

Cambridge Elements ≡

Elements in Applied Social Psychology
edited by
Susan Clayton
College of Wooster, Ohio

TWO OR MORE

A Comparative Analysis of Multiracial and Multicultural Research

Analia F. Albuja
Northeastern University

Alexandria West
Duke University

Sarah E. Gaither
Duke University

CAMBRIDGE
UNIVERSITY PRESS

Shaftesbury Road, Cambridge CB2 8EA, United Kingdom

One Liberty Plaza, 20th Floor, New York, NY 10006, USA

477 Williamstown Road, Port Melbourne, VIC 3207, Australia

314–321, 3rd Floor, Plot 3, Splendor Forum, Jasola District Centre,
New Delhi – 110025, India

103 Penang Road, #05–06/07, Visioncrest Commercial, Singapore 238467

Cambridge University Press is part of Cambridge University Press & Assessment,
a department of the University of Cambridge.

We share the University's mission to contribute to society through the pursuit of
education, learning and research at the highest international levels of excellence.

www.cambridge.org
Information on this title: www.cambridge.org/9781009202718

DOI: 10.1017/9781009202695

© Analia F. Albuja, Alexandria West, and Sarah E. Gaither 2022

This work is in copyright. It is subject to statutory exceptions and to the provisions
of relevant licensing agreements; with the exception of the Creative Commons version
the link for which is provided below, no reproduction of any part of this work may take
place without the written permission of Cambridge University Press & Assessment.

An online version of this work is published at doi.org/10.1017/9781009202695
under a Creative Commons Open Access license CC-BY-NC 4.0 which permits
re-use, distribution and reproduction in any medium for non-commercial purposes
providing appropriate credit to the original work is given and any changes made are
indicated. To view a copy of this license visit https://creativecommons.org/licenses/
by-nc/4.0

All versions of this work may contain content reproduced under license from third
parties. Permission to reproduce this third-party content must be obtained from these
third-parties directly.

When citing this work, please include a reference to the DOI 10.1017/9781009202695

First published 2022

A catalogue record for this publication is available from the British Library.

ISBN 978-1-009-20271-8 Paperback
ISSN 2631-777X (online)
ISSN 2631-7761 (print)

Cambridge University Press & Assessment has no responsibility for the persistence
or accuracy of URLs for external or third-party internet websites referred to in this
publication and does not guarantee that any content on such websites is, or will
remain, accurate or appropriate.

Two or More

A Comparative Analysis of Multiracial and Multicultural Research

Elements in Applied Social Psychology

DOI: 10.1017/9781009202695
First published online: November 2022

Analia F. Albuja
Northeastern University

Alexandria West
Duke University

Sarah E. Gaither
Duke University

Author for correspondence: Analia F. Albuja, a.albuja@northeastern.edu

Abstract: Most research has investigated Multiracial and Multicultural populations as separate topics, despite demographic and experiential overlap between these. This Element bridges that divide by reviewing and comparing Multiracial and Multicultural research to date—their origins, theoretical and methodological development, and key findings in socialization, identity negotiation and discrimination—to identify points of synthesis and differentiation to guide future research. It highlights challenges researchers face when studying these populations because such research topics necessitate that one moves beyond previous frameworks and theories to grapple with identity as flexible, malleable, and influenced both by internal factors and external perceptions. The areas of overlap and difference are meaningful and illustrate the social constructive nature of race and culture, which is always in flux and being re-defined. This title is also available as open access on Cambridge Core.

This Element also has a video abstract: www.cambridge.org/Applied Social Psychology_ Albuja_abstract
Keywords: multiracial, multicultural, discrimination, socialization, identity negotiation

ISBNs: 9781009202718 (PB), 9781009202695 (OC)
ISSNs: 2631-777X (online), 2631-7761 (print)

Contents

1 Introduction   1

2 Historical and Theoretical Foundations   4

3 Methodological Approaches   16

4 Socialization   24

5 Identity Negotiation   31

6 Discrimination   38

7 General Discussion   49

8 Conclusions   55

References   57

1 Introduction

A rise in interracial relationships and increased globalization has ushered in an era of great diversity within the United States. For example, while only 3 percent of married adults in the US were in interracial relationships in 1967, this proportion rose to 11 percent in 2019, including 19 percent of newlyweds (Parker & Barroso, 2021). Similarly, immigrants and descendants of immigrants are projected to account for 88 percent of the total US population growth over the next forty-five years (Pew Research Center, 2015a). This greater diversity includes growing segments of the population that identify as Multiracial or Multicultural, and has engendered greater societal acknowledgment of these groups. Indeed, the Multiracial population grew by 276 percent between 2010 and 2020 (Jones et al., 2021). Here, we use "Multiracial" and "Multicultural" as terms encompassing Biracial and Bicultural individuals. We acknowledge these terms capture very diverse populations, and these groups should not be understood as monoliths. Our goal is to spur additional research to better understand within-group variation of these two rapidly growing demographics through this summary.

Multiracial people are often defined as those whose parents identify with different racial groups (Atkin et al., 2022; Rockquemore et al., 2009). For example, a person with a Black-identified parent and an Asian-identified parent would be considered Multiracial. Some researchers also specify that Multiracial people must self-identify as Multiracial to be considered part of this population. However, Multiracial people's identifications vary, such that some people identify with multiple groups, or as Multiracial, while others identify with only one racial group (Rockquemore et al., 2009; Song, 2021). Moreover, people may also show within-person variation in their identification, changing their identity based on the situational context, or throughout their lifetime (Pew Research Center, 2015b). Because there is no one "correct" way to identify, this identity malleability can create unique research challenges that make researchers contend with nuanced considerations of race, identity, and who is considered Multiracial (see Section 3.1).

Multicultural people are often defined as those who are regularly exposed to and identify with at least two cultures (e.g., first- and second-generation immigrants). Culture is a system of expectations and perspectives shared by a social group that is shaped and passed between members through implicit (e.g., nonverbal approval or disapproval) and explicit means (Boyd & Richeson, 2005; Shweder & Sullivan, 1993). Human groups naturally form their own cultures partly to promote order among members (Boyd & Richerson, 2005; Dunbar, 1998; Geertz, 1973), but also to create a social identity that binds the group together and differentiates them from other groups, providing a sense of belonging that is critical to well-being (Baumeister & Leary, 1995; Deci & Ryan, 2012; Tajfel & Turner, 1979). Any person whose sense of self and related experiences are influenced by the norms, values, and beliefs (i.e., culture) of multiple meaningful social groups could be considered Multicultural (Nguyen & Benet-Martínez, 2007). In reference to a group itself, "culture" can refer to countless types of social categories, and empirically has been studied in many different forms, including not only the more familiar categories of ethnicity and nationality, but also race, religion, socioeconomic status, region, institution, and other meaningful groups (Cohen, 2009; Heine, 2015). Using this broad lens, most people are in some sense bi-, tri-, . . . *n*-cultural (Pekerti et al., 2015). This could serve as a potential bridge between monocultural and Multicultural people. However, much of the past research on Multicultural people has focused on individuals who identify with two cultures. Typically, these have been one mainstream culture (i.e., the culture of the majority group in a given society) and one heritage culture (i.e., the culture of one minority group in a given society), although more recent work has expanded the scope to consider people with more than two cultures (e.g., Downie et al., 2004; Ferguson et al., 2014) and combinations of multiple minority and majority cultures (e.g., West et al., 2021).

1.1 Conceptual Overlap

Given the fast growth of Multiracial and Multicultural populations, research on the psychological and social experiences of these groups has increased (Garay & Remedios, 2021). It is important to note that there may be overlap between these populations both in demographics and self-identification (McFarland & Fingerhut, 2011). For example, a researcher might consider a participant to be both Multiracial and Multicultural based on their operationalization of these terms, or participants themselves may self-identify as both Multiracial and Multicultural. However, most research has either investigated the psychological experiences of Multiracial and Multicultural people separately or has not meaningfully distinguished between the two. The research that has treated these two populations as separate fails to capture how some experiences of identifying with two groups within one identity domain may be shared across domains and not be specific to either holding multiple racial identities or multiple cultural identities. In contrast, research that does not distinguish between these two often operationalizes Multiracial and Multicultural in ways that conflate race and culture. This may obscure nuanced differences in the experience of race and culture.

Notably, these fields have been most integrated in the context of identity socialization, where researchers have observed that people, especially younger populations, do not necessarily differentiate between their racial and cultural identities, and the developmental trajectory of identity socialization is similar for race and culture (Cross & Cross, 2008; Umaña-Taylor et al., 2013). This has culminated in the merging of racial and ethnic socialization into a metaconstruct referred to as ethnic-racial socialization, which has been studied among monoracial racial minorities and Multicultural people (Umaña-Taylor et al., 2013).

1.2 Present Review

However, this integration has not been applied to *Multiracial* and *Multicultural* identity experiences and processes. Therefore, the present work outlines research areas that have been studied among both Multiracial and Multicultural populations, but have often been examined completely separately. For each section, we integrate existing findings to highlight similarities and differences between Multiracial and Multicultural antecedents, processes, and outcomes, and underscore opportunities for future integration and comparison. Consistent with critical race theory's call to challenge ahistoricism and center analyses related to race within a historical context (Harris, 2016; Solórzano & Yosso, 2001), we begin by reviewing the historical tradition and antecedents of research with Multiracial and Multicultural populations. Within this historical context, we then review the methodological approaches used in both traditions to understand researchers' processes in this work. Next, we compare research on socialization, identity negotiation, and discrimination between Multiracial and Multicultural populations, as these topics have received wide attention across disciplines and are central outcomes of the multiracial and multicultural experience. Within each section, we review the literature on each population broadly across psychological, sociological, educational, and social work disciplines, among others, and integrate the findings, first for Multiracial populations and second for Multicultural populations. Each section concludes with a systematic comparison and integration across populations, with the goal of elucidating areas of overlap and distinction to encourage nuanced consideration of multiraciality and multiculturalism in future research.

This Element integrates the existing literatures focusing on Multiracial and Multicultural people to highlight both similarities and differences between these populations, and the methods used to study them. We believe all researchers, even those whose research specialization does not include the study of these populations, have much to learn from the study of Multiracial and Multicultural populations. Given cognitive, academic, and societal preferences for singular and fixed understandings of identity, the experiences of Multiracial and Multicultural people are unique and demand that we extend our thinking of identity to be broader and more flexible. This Element will demonstrate how, compared to monoracial and monocultural people, the history of Multiracial and Multicultural people in the US is unique, how these populations in particular pose distinct research challenges, and how Multiracial and Multicultural people may be socialized about race differently, in addition to discussing how negotiating multiple racial and cultural identities leads to unique experiences of discrimination. By acknowledging these differences, and focusing specifically on the overlap between these two populations, we will highlight how the boundaries of research on race, culture, and identity must expand to accurately understand and represent the diversity of experience in the US. Furthermore, the quick growth of these populations underscores the importance of this research, as growing numbers of people continue to be underrepresented and poorly understood in academic research. Finally, this Element holds important implications and applications for researchers, practitioners, and policymakers as the Multiracial and Multicultural populations in the US continue to grow. For example, this work would be informative to decision makers involved in processes such as designing and interpreting the US census, making health care more equitable, and legislating citizenship (Sanchez et al., 2020; Verkuyten, 2018).

2 Historical and Theoretical Foundations

Understanding the contemporary experiences of the Multiracial and Multicultural communities in the US requires contextualizing the present through a historical perspective (Harris, 2016). Because research on the experiences of Multiracial and Multicultural people has been influenced by societal perceptions of these populations, it is important to first examine how multiraciality and multiculturalism have been conceptualized and treated throughout US history to understand the historical and theoretical foundations of this work.

Although a relatively new topic in psychology, other social sciences have a longer tradition of considering the unique experiences of people who straddle multiple worlds of race and culture. For example, venerated sociologist and historian, W. E. B. Du Bois observed the "double consciousness" experiences of Black Americans in the late 1800s and early 1900s, whereby the separation and hierarchy of their Black versus mainstream American cultural worlds was internalized as a rift in the self, a "two-ness" that threatens to pull the individual apart (1903). Placing Du Bois' phenomenon in its sociohistorical context of post-civil war, pre-civil rights in the US also evokes consideration of the role of broader societal attitudes and beliefs in shaping the multiracial and multicultural experiences. Such insights help root current psychological work in the perspectives and lived experiences of Multiracial and Multicultural people, drawing on accounts of what it is like to negotiate multiple races and cultures, rather than assuming what it may be like from an outside observer perspective. Understanding current work requires examining the impact of the sociohistorical context on Multiracial and Multicultural populations and research with these groups.

2.1 Multiracial People throughout US History

Multiraciality is not a novel phenomenon, as Multiracial people have been part of the early history of the US and other countries. This section focuses on the history and psychological theorizing about Multiracial people in the US because specific historical circumstances (i.e., the role of slavery in racial definitions) have led to most research on the multiracial experience focusing on US Multiracial people, especially Multiracial people who have White ancestry (Garay & Remedios, 2021; Ifekwunigwe, 2004; Nobles, 2000; Song, 2021). As such, we do not generalize these historical foundations to other countries.

The multiracial experience in the US has been shaped by historical and current sociopolitical forces. Although racial mixing began as early as colonial settlers interacted with Native Americans, controlling race and racial identification was key to owning property, gaining wealth, and maintaining slavery and segregation (Carter, 2013; Davis, 1991). For example, Thomas Jefferson's *Notes on Virginia* advocated against racial mixing, and anti-miscegenation laws banning interracial marriage were enacted in the seventeenth-century colonies (Davis, 1991; Wallenstein, 2004). Ultimately, thirty states had anti-miscegenation laws (American Civil Liberties Union, n.d.). States varied in which racial groups they prohibited from marriage, underscoring the prejudicial motivation that targeted specific racial minorities based on their regional representation (Browning, 1951; Sohoni, 2007).

Despite this legislation, interracial relationships continued, including those between White indentured servants and freed Black people in the Upper South, and those forced onto enslaved Black women by White slave owners in the Lower South (Davis, 1991). Because the Multiracial offspring of these relationships complicated determinations of who was free and who was enslaved, attitudes toward racial mixing often mirrored attitudes toward slavery (Carter, 2013). The racial hierarchy was further threatened by the end of slavery. Thus, to justify and maintain the White supremacist hierarchy, Multiracial identity was scrutinized and controlled through the US census (Bennett, 2000; Hochschild & Powell, 2008). Between 1850 and 1930, the US census experimented broadly with racial categories, leading to inconsistent and unstable population estimates during these years (Hochschild & Powell, 2008). For example, in 1850, the scope of the US census expanded from enumerating free and enslaved people to gathering more detailed information about each person to support racist arguments justifying the enslavement of Black people. As a result, the category "mulatto" was included, which was identified by skin tone and used to demonstrate the purported negative consequences of racial mixing (Hochschild & Powell, 2008). By 1890, subcategories of "mulatto" appeared on the census, categorizing people based on their fraction of "Black blood" (Hochschild & Powell, 2008).

These categories were dropped from the census after 1920 because they were deemed statistically unreliable, and because of political pressure. For example, Du Bois advocated against a separate census category for Multiracial people, as he believed that it would weaken solidarity within a White supremacist system. Consequently, the one-drop rule became uniformly accepted in the 1920s (Davis, 1991). The one-drop rule, also referred to as hypodescent, categorized people who had any Black ancestry as Black, though it eventually spread to categorize anyone who had non-White ancestry as members of their racial minority group (Davis, 1991; Sohoni, 2007; Thompson, 2012). This categorization persisted during the Jim Crow period, serving to enforce segregation (Davis, 1991).

Despite consistent politicization of Multiracial identification, Multiracial people often resisted attempts to control their identity. For example, many Multiracial people passed as White, or incorporated themselves into White community permanently or briefly, in order to secure better jobs and increase their safety (Daniel, 1992). Passing may have only been accessible to Multiracial people with ambiguous phenotypic presentation. A legal challenge to anti-miscegenation laws brought forward by a Black and White interracial couple led to the end of bans on interracial marriage in the 1967 *Loving v. Virginia* Supreme Court ruling (Lombardo, 1988). Since then, public opinion toward interracial marriage has become more positive, with as many as 87 percent of respondents to a Gallup poll approving of marriage between Black and White people (Saad, 2017). Multiracial people's resistance is also seen through advocacy for formal recognition of Multiracial people in the US census in the 1990s (Thompson, 2012). For example, 500,000 people selected two or more responses in the 1990 census in protest of the instructions forcing only one choice (Wallman et al., 2000). Despite political pressure from civil rights activists such as Jesse Jackson, who argued that allowing multiple racial identifications would dilute the Census Bureau's ability to document racial disparities, Multiracial activists from organizations such as RACE (Reclassify All Children Equally) successfully lobbied for the allowance of selecting multiple racial options on the census (Rockquemore & Brunsma, 2002; Snipp, 2003). This change began with the 2000 census (Williams, 2006).

2.2 History of the Study of Multiracial People

2.2.1 Deficit Perspective

The study of Multiracial people often parallels the sociopolitical zeitgeist surrounding this population (Kahn & Denmon, 1997). Multiracial identity development models began from a deficit perspective, positing that Multiracial people had a fragmented sense of self and were heavily marginalized (Brandell, 1988; Gibbs & Moskowitz-Sweet, 1991; Herring, 1995; McRoy & Freeman, 1986; Park, 1928, 1931; Stonequist, 1937; Thornton, 1996). Because most of this research studied Multiracial people with Black and White ancestry, the prevailing view concluded that it was problematic for someone to incorporate these two groups, given the perceived vast differences in values and attitudes (Thornton, 1996). Within this bipolar view, people could only identify with either one racial group or the other. Maintaining ties to only one group was perceived to be a healthier approach than maintaining ties with both groups (Thornton, 1996; Wardle, 1987). Nonetheless, the marginal man hypothesis posited that Multiracial people are on the margins of *both* racial groups they identify with, and are never fully accepted into either (Park, 1928; Stonequist, 1937). Evidence to support this view was often drawn from clinical samples (Shih & Sanchez, 2005; Thornton, 1996).

2.2.2 Equivalent Approach

While the deficit approach focused primarily on the struggles Multiracial people may face, painting them as inevitable and insurmountable, other theories evolved that incorporated a more diverse range of experiences (Cross, 1987; Porter & Washington, 1993). These were modeled after monoracial identity development models, and incorporated Erikson's (1968) perspective that adolescence is a time to seek stability (Field, 1996; Kerwin et al., 1993). Thus, the next phase of Multiracial identity development models often compared outcomes between Multiracial adolescents and their monoracial counterparts (Campbell & Eggerling-Boeck, 2006; Cooney & Radina, 2000; Grove, 1991; Johnson & Nagoshi, 1986). These studies positioned differences among Multiracial populations as deviant from the monoracial developmental norm.

This work often showed small or no differences between monoracial and Multiracial people (e.g., Campbell & Eggerling-Boeck, 2006), thus negating the deficit perspective from earlier eras.

2.2.3 Variant Approach

Identity development models specific to Multiracial people were developed to expand upon the equivalence approach (Collins, 2000; Kerwin et al., 1993; Kich, 1992; Poston, 1990; Wijeyesinghe, 2001; Williams, 1999). This era of research acknowledged Multiracial people as a separate racial group that required unique theoretical understanding (Shih & Sanchez, 2005). The models developed to understand Multiracial identification generally describe a multistep or multifactor process that begins with confusion and conflict between one's multiple identities, and concludes with acceptance and integration of the multiple groups. While some conclude with a Multiracial identity (e.g., Kich, 1992; Poston, 1990), others acknowledge that racial identity may vary by person (Wijeyesinghe, 2001). This theorizing coincided with growing numbers of people who identified with multiple backgrounds and the advancement of the multiracial advocacy movement (Wijeyesinghe, 2001).

2.2.4 Ecological Approach

The models from the variant approach have evolved to include ecological approaches by specifying that the stages are not necessarily linear and may be influenced by the external environment (Csizmadia, 2011; Rockquemore & Lazloffy, 2005; Rockquemore et al., 2009; Root, 2003; Tomishima, 1999). The ecological view also proposes that Multiracial identity is variable across the population (Rockquemore et al., 2009). For example, some Multiracial people identify with a singular identity, while others may identify with both groups, identify as "Multiracial," or alternate between different identity options (Rockquemore et al., 2009). In addition to variation within the population, identity also changes over the course of a lifetime and is influenced by contextual factors (Rockquemore et al., 2009). The ecological approach considers these many sources of variation.

2.2.5 Critical Race Approach

Finally, a critical race perspective has emerged. The field of "mixed race studies" began with the publication of three influential edited collections: *Racially Mixed People in America* (Root, 1992), *The Multiracial Experience* (Root, 1996), and *Race and Mixed Race* (Zack, 1994). Root's (1996) "Bill of

Rights" for Multiracial people demonstrated their resilience in the face of sociopolitical control over their identities, and has ushered in greater acceptance of this population (Charmaraman et al., 2014). This publication was foundational to the multiracial movement that advocated for the freedom to choose one's identity, as seen through the advocacy for multiple choice options on the census (American Psychological Association, 2006). Later waves of mixed race studies consider the role of political and economic power structures in shaping definitions of Multiracial identity, extend beyond the Black/White binary, and incorporate additional social identities (Ifekwunigwe, 2004; Rockquemore & Brunsma, 2002; Williams-León & Nakashima, 2001). Moreover, MultiCrit theory has drawn from critical race theory to create a critical theoretical perspective that is specific to multiracial experiences (Harris, 2016). The core tenets of MultiCrit challenge ahistoric approaches that ignore relevant sociopolitical historical context, acknowledge the convergence of outside interests in shaping Multiracial people's experiences, and center Multiracial people's narratives to challenge White supremacy (Harris, 2016). This work also focuses on Multiracial people's experiences of discrimination, particularly as they navigate a society designed for monoracial people (Johnston & Nadal, 2010).

2.3 Multicultural People Throughout US History

The early twentieth century was characterized by mass migration in the US, leading the foreign-born population to account for 12–15 percent of the US population between 1880 and 1930 (Birman & Simon, 2014; Grieco, 2014). The Chinese population within the US tripled between 1860 and 1890, and the Japanese population grew from 2,000 people in 1890 to over 70,000 in 1920 (Sohoni, 2007). Alongside this influx of immigration came legislation restricting immigration and naturalization, which excluded these populations from full participation in mainstream culture (Sohoni, 2007). For example, the 1875 Naturalization Act only allowed naturalization for White and African Americans, and the 1882 Chinese Exclusion Act restricted immigration from China (Sohoni, 2007). In order to classify the growing immigrant populations, by 1930 there were US census categories for Mexican, Filipino, Hindu, and Korean (Snipp, 2003). Though immigration decreased by the 1970s, the "Second Great Wave" of immigration began after the 1970s, leading to a 400 percent increase in the foreign-born population by 2010 and comprising 14.8 percent of the population by 2019 (Batalova et al., 2021; Grieco, 2014).

Within this zeitgeist, social scientific research began studying immigrant populations, primarily using the framework of acculturation (Birman & Simon, 2014). Indeed, beginning as early as 1918 with Thomas and

Znaniecki's publication of *The Polish Peasant in Europe and America*, theories of multiculturalism were rooted in acculturation research, which examines how people adapt individually, interpersonally, and at a group level as a result of continuous and direct contact with others from diverse cultural groups (Berry et al., 2006; Redfield et al., 1936; Rudmin et al., 2017). Early models of acculturation posited that only "primitive" people acculturate after encountering "advanced" people, while those "advanced" people do not acculturate (Rudmin et al., 2017). Later models noted that acculturation is a bidirectional process where both local and immigrant populations may acculturate (Kunst et al., 2021; Redfield et al., 1936). Models of Multicultural people's identity usually proposed that individuals maintained (1) a singular cultural identity (either their mainstream or their heritage group; e.g., an Ecuadorian immigrant to the US identifying only as Ecuadorian or only as American) or (2) both mainstream and heritage cultural identities (see Ryder et al., 2000; e.g., an Ecuadorian immigrant to the US identifying as Ecuadorian and American, or as Ecuadorian-American). Later multiculturalism theories focused on people who identify with both mainstream and heritage cultural identities and provided insight into the processes people use to maintain their two cultures.

2.4 History of the Study of Multicultural People

2.4.1 Additive Models

Acculturation has typically been conceived as either a unidimensional or a bidimensional process. In the unidimensional framework of acculturation, one would move from membership in their heritage culture (separation) to membership in their majority culture (assimilation) or vice versa (Birman & Simon, 2014; West et al., 2017). In this way, the unidimensional model conceived of cultural identity as a zero-sum experience in which one must lose one cultural identity to identify with another cultural group (e.g., Gordon, 1964; Suinn et al., 1987). In contrast, the bidimensional model conceived of one's cultural adaptation along two parallel lines of majority and heritage cultural involvement, respectively. In addition to the assimilation and separation identity patterns, it is also possible to display a marginalized orientation, or disidentify with both groups. Finally, the most studied configuration is integration, or biculturalism, in which one simultaneously maintains membership in both heritage and mainstream cultural groups (Berry, 1980, 1997; Berry et al., 2006; Ryder et al., 2000). In this model, cultural identification is seen as bidimensional in that one can have a second identity without losing the first, but it is still ultimately additive because the sum of identification with each culture determines one's identity.

There are several limitations to the unidimensional and bidimensional models. For example, both frameworks tend to consider only two cultures that are dichotomized according to mainstream and heritage status, and treat cultural identities as independent from one another (see Rudmin, 2003). In response to those critiques, researchers have developed a tridimensional model of acculturation, which measures people's orientation toward their heritage culture, the dominant culture, and a third culture (Ferguson, 2013; Ferguson et al., 2012, 2014; Ozer & Schwartz, 2016). For example, Chinese mothers in the US were orientated toward Chinese, American, and Chinese-American culture as three separate cultural orientations (Kim & Hou, 2016). Similarly, Ladakhi adults living in Ladakh or in Indian cities such as Delhi demonstrated tridimensional acculturation toward Ladakhi, Indian, and Western cultures (Ozer & Schwartz, 2016). The tridimensional model may better capture the complexities of acculturation within a globalized context. Moreover, the unidimensional and bidimensional models cast Multicultural people in a passive role as recipients of their monolithic cultures rather than as active participants who are constantly interpreting, forming, and reforming their understanding of their cultures and the role they play in their evolving understanding of themselves and their world. Mounting research provides evidence that Multicultural people's identities are multifaceted, interrelated, and dynamic (see Doucerain et al., 2013; van Oudenhoven & Benet-Martínez, 2015; Yampolsky et al., 2013; Zhang et al., 2014), which leads the next era of researchers to propose more dynamic models of Multicultural identity (Vertovec, 2007).

2.4.2 Dynamic Models

Multiculturalism research has begun providing needed insight into the diverse ways that Multicultural people experience their cultures and the variety of skills and appraisals that shape the nature of these experiences. In one of the field's watershed publications, Hong and colleagues (2000) put forth a dynamic constructivist model of multicultural cognition that provided evidence that the effects of a person's cultures are neither static nor passively received. Rather, Multicultural people are active agents who draw on their cultures differently as functions of situational and individual factors. As evidence of this dynamism in action, cultural frame switching was developed to capture Multicultural people's experience of adapting to situationally salient cultural contexts by activating cultural systems of knowledge (Hong et al., 2000). The observance of cultural frame switching challenged and extended previous additive theories in two important ways. First, it drew on knowledge activation research (Higgins, 1996) to explain how cultural knowledge follows the same basic cognitive principles of activation as any knowledge structure. Thus, the frame-switching model provides a person-by-situation analytic framework in which a subset of one's cultural knowledge is cued by the immediate environment and subsequently serves as a behavioral guide. The implication is that Multicultural people can acquire multiple knowledge structures, but these take turns to become operative and guide action. Second, in the lived experience of many Multicultural people, frame switching is likely rooted in the relative separateness of life domains. For example, host culture likely dominates in public domains, and heritage culture likely dominates in private domains (Arends-Tóth & van de Vijver, 2004). Thus, frame switching is one functional process Multicultural people may use to balance their dual-cultural orientations in everyday life.

Rooted in the same dynamic constructivist model, Benet-Martínez and colleagues went on to identify an internal source of variance and complexity that modulates the effects of a Multicultural person's cultures – their idiosyncratic appraisal of the relationship between their cultures (Benet-Martínez & Haritatos, 2005). Researchers noticed that Multicultural individuals differ in the way they cognitively and behaviorally react to the same cultural context, with some Multicultural people assimilating themselves to the salient culture and others contrasting away from that culture by adopting culturally atypical thoughts and behaviors (Benet-Martínez et al., 2002; Friedman et al., 2012; Mok & Morris, 2009, 2013). This range of responses was reliably associated with a Multicultural person's sense of Bicultural identity integration, or their appraisal of similarity and harmony between their cultures (Benet-Martínez & Haritatos, 2005; Mok & Morris, 2013). Multicultural people with high Bicultural identity integration view their cultural identities as compatible and overlapping, while those with low identity integration view their cultural identities as conflicting and separated (Benet-Martínez & Haritatos, 2005; Huynh et al., 2011). Multicultural people high in identity integration assimilated their behavior to the primed culture, while Multicultural people low in identity integration contrasted their behavior away from the primed culture by adopting behavior more characteristic of their nonprimed culture.

Further research went on to show that Multicultural people's appraisals of cultural integration not only shaped the effects of any single culture, but also impacted the effects of having multicultural experiences and identities. Increasingly, studies have documented the transformative ways that experiencing and negotiating multiple cultures can alter a person, identifying what West and colleagues refer to as "unique products of biculturalism": psychological characteristics that differ in degree or type from monocultural people. For example, cultural frame switching and Bicultural identity integration are linked to greater cognitive complexity in Multicultural people's cultural representations (Benet-Martínez et al., 2006), and these unique products seem to manifest in Multicultural people's behavior and cognition more broadly as well. For instance, Multicultural people with more integrated identities show greater integrative complexity, acknowledging conflicting perspectives and using more complex solutions to resolve conflict in cultural and work domains (Tadmor et al., 2009), and their enhanced integrative complexity predicts greater creativity (Tadmor, Galinsky, et al., 2012). In addition, individual differences, such as a greater tolerance of uncertainty, seem to facilitate the effects of multicultural exposure on lower intergroup biases (Tadmor, Hong, et al., 2012). Together, the dynamic models greatly advanced appreciation of the diversity among Multicultural people and how they are impacted by their cultures differently according to situational, personal, and situation × person interactive factors. This research shifted the nature of the Multicultural person to an active agent who has some control over how they respond to their cultures and identified multiple skills and appraisals that shape Multicultural peoples' responses.

2.4.3 Process-Focused Models

A new epoch of process-focused theories of multiculturalism has emerged in which the processes Multicultural people use to navigate their cultures is a major focus (Meca et al., 2019; Sam & Ward, 2021; Ward et al., 2018). Process-focused theories bring attention to the cognitive and behavioral processes that underlie the prior dynamic models' key discoveries. For instance, in considering that Multicultural people vary in their level of identity integration, researchers are asking how a person comes to view their cultures as integrated, emphasizing the various active approaches a Multicultural person enacts in order to achieve high integration. For example, Ward and colleagues (2018) posit that selectively employing one cultural identity over another (i.e., alternating identity style) versus drawing on a merged identity that reflects a mix of multiple cultures (i.e., hybridizing identity style) are two distinct strategies Multicultural people use toward the end goal of integrating their identities. Identifying and differentiating between these processes that facilitate multiple cultural identity negotiation can deepen our understanding of why the heterogeneity of multicultural experiences occurs.

Furthermore, process-focused models build on the dynamic approach by emphasizing the importance of the skills and appraisals that enable Multicultural people to negotiate their multiple cultures, reframing these cognitive and behavioral processes as factors that not only moderate the effects of cultures, but also cause the effects of being Multicultural. For instance, in reference to the benefits of multicultural experience on creativity, a process-focused model might probe further into the augmenting role of higher identity integration as a causal mechanism of multicultural creativity. It would be informative for future research to test whether experiencing multiple cultures fosters creativity because the process of integrating cultural identities causes a person to become more creative.

A key process-focused theory is the transformative theory of multicultur-alism, which posits that Multicultural people's characteristics and experiences result not only from the direct influences of each of their cultures, but also from the processes they use to negotiate their cultures (e.g., frame switching; West et al., 2017). To illustrate, recent work finds that one reason why Multicultural people are regarded with suspicion and distrust by White majority monocultural people is not only the mere fact that they hold multiple cultural identities, but specifically because of their cultural frame-switching behavior (West et al., 2017, 2021). This transformative approach emphasizes that both the diversity and commonalities of Multicultural people's lived experiences that differentiate them from their monocultural peers can be better understood by studying how the use of different strategies to manage one's multiple cultures affects Multicultural people psychologically and socially. Future research should study how the process of identity negotiation leads to other unique multicultural products, such as resilience, and confron-tation of discrimination. For example, the skills Multicultural people gain through the process of frame-switching could lead to unique responses to discrimination.

2.5 Comparing Historical and Theoretical Foundations

Theoretical approaches to research on Multiracial and Multicultural populations have changed over time. For both populations, early conceptualization was centered on Multiracial and Multicultural people selecting only one identity, primarily the lower status identity. In the case of Multiracial identity, status differences between White and Black people in the US were perceived to be too vast to successfully integrate into one identity (Thornton, 1996). Similarly, given the xenophobic roots of acculturation theory (Rudmin et al., 2017), research on Multicultural identity also began from a unidimensional perspective where Multicultural people were perceived to only identify with one end of a bipolar distribution (Rudmin, 2003). For Multiracial people, this view fol-lowed from hypodescent norms while for Multicultural people it stemmed from increased globalization. Nonetheless, these two traditions share the initial theoretical approach that sought to apply monoracial or monocultural norms and expectations to Multiracial and Multicultural populations.

Later theoretical developments incorporated dynamic and ecological perspectives to understanding Multiracial and Multicultural identity. For both populations, this involved acknowledging how situations make racial or cultural identities more accessible, and minimized the perception that there is one optimal "endpoint" for Multiracial or Multicultural identity development (Rockquemore et al., 2009). Among Multiracial populations, most of this work examined identity change longitudinally over the course of two to ten years, including several studies using the National Longitudinal Study of Adolescent to Adult Health (DeFina & Hannon 2016; Doyle & Kao, 2007; Hitlin et al., 2006; Liebler et al., 2017; Reece, 2019; see Wilton et al., 2013 for a study using daily diary methodology), or through self-report of identity fluidity (e.g., Lou et al., 2011; Lou & Lalonde, 2015; Lusk et al., 2010; Rockquemore & Arend, 2002; Rockquemore & Brunsma, 2004; Sanchez et al., 2009), while relatively less work has tested different situations within one timepoint (e.g., Chiao et al., 2006; Gaither et al., 2013; Gaither, Cohen-Goldberg, et al., 2015; Gaither, Remedios, et al., 2015; Harris & Sim, 2002; Pauker et al., 2013). This perspective highlights how factors such as gender, socioeconomic status, and phenotype influence the likelihood and directionality of racial identity change, rather than situational accessibility of racial identity schemas. In contrast, research among Multicultural populations has examined identity change in the moment after exposure to a laboratory cultural prime (e.g., Benet-Martínez et al., 2002; Mok & Morris, 2009; Ramirez-Esparza et al., 2006; Verkuyten & Pouliasi, 2006), as well as longitudinally (e.g., Matsunaga et al., 2010; Schwartz et al., 2015; Tartakovsky, 2009). This work identified gender, socioeconomic status, and immigration status as relevant factors to identity fluidity. Taken together, identity fluidity may be a shared experience across both Multiracial and Multicultural populations, though currently less research has examined the situational access to different racial identities elicited through experimental designs among Multiracial people.

While multiracial research also included an equivalent approach, where Multiracial and monoracial people were directly compared on outcomes such as social adjustment and well-being (Campbell & Eggerling-Boeck, 2006), multicultural research has focused less on direct comparisons between Multicultural and monocultural people. Rather, much research has focused on differences in outcomes among Multicultural people with different identity profiles (Schwartz et al., 2015). Within the context of race, monoracial identity is seen as the norm and is supported socially and institutionally, leaving multiraciality to be positioned as deviant, and understood relative to monoracial benchmarks (Harris, 2016). Given more expansive definitions of multicultural-ism, and the historical roots of this research tradition in understanding different patterns of response to immigration, research on Multicultural populations has seen less of an equivalent approach.

Finally, the latest developments in multiracial theorizing take a critical race approach that acknowledges systemic issues and demonstrates how multiraci-ality is shaped by power structures (Harris, 2016). In contrast, the latest developments in multicultural theorizing focus on processes of identity negoti-ation, considering how internal and individual approaches to identity shape those identities rather than systemic structures (West et al., 2017). Future research would benefit from a blend of these approaches that considers both how individual choices and internal processes are shaped by structural and external forces, interacting to create Multiracial and Multicultural identities that are not only internally dynamic, but externally dynamic as well. For example, studies exploring identity fluidity may incorporate both daily diary methodology to account for within-person differences in factors such as a sense of belonging, and longitudinal methodology to assess changes over time. Moreover, recruiting participants from across the US would further allow for the incorporation of neighborhood variables such as racial composition.

3 Methodological Approaches

Increased research on Multiracial and Multicultural populations has not only included theoretical advancements but also methodological advancements (Root, 2002). Methodological approaches incorporate both qualitative and quantitative methods focusing on a variety of questions. This work extends beyond previous methods used to study race and culture by tackling challenges such as designing inclusion criteria that represent these populations and account for malleable identification. Despite significant progress, several methodo-logical limitations hinder greater representation of this research.

3.1 Methodological Approach of Multiracial Research

Alongside theoretical developments focused on Multiracial populations, meth-odological approaches have similarly evolved. A content review of research on Multiracial people between 1990 and 2009 identified 133 studies, demonstrat-ing growing research interest in this population (Charmaraman et al., 2014). The majority (69 percent) of research during this time was quantitative, though earlier research was more likely to be qualitative, including case studies and observational studies of support groups for Multiracial people (Charmaraman et al., 2014; Rockquemore et al., 2009; Shih & Sanchez, 2005). Similarly, a 2005 review of Multiracial people's identity development and well-being across relationships, school outcomes, and self-esteem identified more qualitative studies than quantitative studies (twenty-eight compared to fifteen), demonstrating an earlier focus on qualitative work (Shih & Sanchez, 2005). Yet, a content analysis within counseling psychology up to 2006 revealed equal numbers of qualitative and quantitative studies, suggesting heterogeneity of approaches by subfield (Edwards & Pedrotti, 2008). The growth of quantitative research has been propelled by an increased availability of large-scale surveys that include information about parents' race, such as the National Longitudinal Study of Adolescent Health (Rockquemore et al., 2009).

The most frequently studied topics have been racial identity and phenotypic presentation, with many studies focusing on how Multiracial people categorize themselves and are categorized by others based on their phenotype (Charmaraman et al., 2014; Edwards & Pedrotti, 2008; Miville, 2005). A review of experimental multiracial research within social psychology between 2000 and 2020 identified racial categorization, interracial interactions, and experiences of Multiracial people as the most frequently studied topics (Garay & Remedios, 2021). Studies of how Multiracial people are categorized by others have demonstrated that perceptions of Multiracial people differ based on perceivers' racial and political ideology, racial attitudes, and racial identity (Chao et al., 2013; Eberhardt et al., 2003; Gaither et al., 2016; Ho et al., 2013, 2015; Hugenberg & Bodenhausen, 2004; Krosch et al., 2013; Kteily et al., 2014; see Pauker, Meyers, et al., 2018 for a review). For example, the Sociopolitical Motive × Intergroup Threat Model posits that categorization of Multiracial people is influenced by people's perceptions of threat to the hierarchy and to ingroup norms, such that high status group members are more likely to categorize Multiracial people as outgroup members in instances of high hierarchy and group norm threat (Ho et al., 2020). Categorization can also be influenced by the targets' gender, racial identity, phenotype, and socioeconomic status (Freeman et al., 2011; MacLin & Malpass, 2001; Pauker, Carpinella et al., 2018). Finally, contextual factors such as exposure to racial diversity, economic scarcity, and group threat can also influence categorization of Multiracial faces (Dickter & Kittel, 2012; Freeman et al., 2016; Krosch & Amodio, 2014; Krosch et al., 2022; Rodeheffer et al., 2012). This work has shown that Multiracial people can be categorized as members of their lower status group (i.e., according to hypodescent), as a minority group member that is not part of their ancestry, or as Multiracial (see Chen, 2019 for a review). A meta-analytic review also demonstrates the importance of methodological decisions, as evidence of hypodescent was only seen when multiraciality was operationalized through ancestry information, the target of categorization was male, and categorization was done through multiple Likert scales or through a dichotomous outcome (Young et al., 2021). Across this research, several methodological challenges arose, particularly surrounding how to define and measure Multiracial populations in ways that are responsive to people's own self-identification and to the fluidity of racial identity.

3.1.1 Challenges in Defining Multiracial People

A central challenge in the research of Multiracial people is how these populations are defined. As reviewed, inclusion within the Multiracial category is heavily influenced by sociopolitical factors (Song, 2021). Because of this heterogeneity, research on Multiracial people has used vastly different definitions of the population across research labs and historical time (Edwards & Pedrotti, 2008).

Researchers' challenges in defining Multiracial people are further complicated by participants' own various self-identifications. Multiracial classification is often assessed by applying monoracial frameworks to Multiracial populations, but this does not account for the unique aspects of Multiracial identity (Woo et al., 2011). For example, monoracial frameworks rarely consider a possible discrepancy between self-identification and others' identification. Yet, this is a common occurrence for Multiracial people, with evidence indicating that people may be misidentified in systematic ways that correlate with social status (Saperstein & Penner, 2012).

To account for these unique experiences of Multiracial people, some researchers have conceptualized multiracial status as a multidimensional construct that includes mixed genealogical ancestry, self-identification, and socially assigned status (Woo et al., 2011). Similarly, Rockquemore et al. (2009) differentiated between people's own self-identification (referred to as racial identity), other's identification of the person (i.e., racial identification), and the availability of racial options in a given context (i.e., racial category). Finally, another typology includes observed race based on appearance and interactions, phenotype, and the race people believe they are seen as (referred to as reflected race) in addition to self-identification and self-classification based on the context and racial ancestry (Roth, 2016). This perspective highlights the possibility of people for whom these categories do not always overlap.

These conceptualizations are consequential for how multiracial status is measured. For example, the US census relies on racial categories to enumerate the Multiracial population rather than racial identity (Rockquemore et al., 2009). In contrast, lay perceivers rely on racial ancestry when enumerating Multiracial people. For example, participants expected that others were more likely to categorize a Black-White Biracial target as Black if the target had greater Black ancestry, and were themselves more likely to categorize a Black-White Biracial target as Black if the target had greater Black ancestry, though this effect was weaker (Sanchez et al., 2011). Among researchers, most studies (65 percent) between 1990 and 2009 presented participants with a single identification measure, though there was variation in the identification format (Charmaraman et al., 2014). Some studies (28 percent) allowed respondents to select multiple racial identification options, while others used qualitative interviews or allowed respondents to identify with a Biracial, Multiracial or mixed category (Charmaraman et al., 2014). Researchers must then also make decisions about how to aggregate such data and into how many Multiracial subcategories, as these decisions may accentuate or minimize group differences in health and education (Gigli, 2021; Herman, 2020).

Further, these inclusion criteria may not be a methodologically responsive approach to research with this population because a key aspect of Multiracial identity is experiencing fluidity in one's identity (Rockquemore, 1999). Indeed, racial identification has been demonstrated to change situationally and over the life course (Davenport, 2016; Liebler et al., 2017; Pew Research Center, 2015b). For example, 9.8 million people reported a difference race or ethnicity between the 2000 and 2010 censuses (Liebler et al., 2017). To account for this fluidity, Rockquemore (1999) developed a taxonomy of racial identity for Black-White Multiracial people, which includes (1) singular (identify only as Black or only as White), (2) border (identify only as Biracial), (3) protean (alternate between Black, White, and Biracial identities), and (4) transcendent (do not identify with any racial group) identities. This approach allows researchers to assess identity fluidity through the protean identity. Other researchers have recommended a two-step approach whereby participants first report their parents' race and then self-identify, thus removing the necessity of self-identification as Multiracial because that can be fluid (Woo et al., 2011).

Across these various methodological approaches to identifying and studying Multiracial populations, the generalizability of the existing work is hindered by several limitations. For example, a recurring practice is the centering of Whiteness within this work, as seen through the overrepresentation of White ancestry in multiracial study samples. Indeed, between 2000 and 2020, 87 percent of Multiracial participants in experimental social psychological research reported White ancestry (Garay & Remedios, 2021). Similarly, most Multiracial participants in reviews of earlier multiracial research reported White ancestry (Charmaraman et al., 2014; Edwards & Pedrotti, 2008). There has also been limited geographic distribution within this research, as most studies have been conducted in the US, and typically within one region of the US (Charmaraman et al., 2014). This methodological approach limits the conclusions and generalizations of the existing literature, as Whiteness plays a different role in upholding the existing status quo for minoritized populations who do not have White ancestry (Garay & Remedios, 2021).

3.2 Methodological Approach of Multicultural Research

A highly studied topic with multicultural samples is the process of acculturation (Chirkov, 2009). Indeed, approximately 6,000 studies on acculturation were conducted in the last decade alone (Rudmin et al., 2017). A review of forty-two articles in leading journals in the study of acculturation demonstrated that most studies were empirical (95 percent of articles) and correlational (82.5 percent of articles) and only one article included qualitative methodology (Chirkov, 2009). This methodological approach reflects a universalist perspective adopted by many acculturation researchers, which indicates that acculturation processes occur similarly across different groups (Berry, 2009; Berry & Sam, 1997). Critics of this approach have employed different frameworks, such as liberation psychology (i.e., a clinical and academic approach that prioritizes oppressed populations) by incorporating individual empowerment processes into acculturation (García-Ramírez et al., 2011). Meta-analyses with broader search criteria have also identified qualitative studies on the association between acculturation and psychological adjustment among students (Makarova & Birman, 2016). Most often, acculturation research focuses on cultural identity as the medium for cultural orientation, and includes various outcomes such as health and academic achievement (Chirkov, 2009; Makarova & Birman, 2015).

Various critiques of acculturation research claim there is an inconsistent use of methods and constructs across the literature that prohibits researchers from drawing broad conclusions across studies, particularly with regards to how acculturation relates to health outcomes (Birman & Simon, 2014; Koneru et al., 2007; Rudmin, 2009; Rudmin et al., 2017). For example, several definitions of acculturation exist, leading to different operationalizations across studies, including frequent use of proxy measures (e.g., country of birth and length of time in the US) rather than direct measures of acculturation (Birman & Simon, 2014). Moreover, researchers continue to use unilinear measures (e.g., asking participants which language they use the most) rather than bilinear measures despite a theoretical shift to understanding acculturation as bilinear (Birman & Simon, 2014). Finally, acculturation research often confounds dimensions of acculturation, such as measuring which culture Multicultural people participate in most, which could represent language, behavior, attitudes, or identity (Birman & Simon, 2014; Schwartz et al., 2010). Similarly, past work has been critiqued for other important confounds that are not often accounted for, including socioeconomic status, or using large pan-ethnic groups of participants and failing to examine subgroup differences, such as differences in acculturation between Latinx Americans from different countries (Birman & Simon, 2014; Rudmin, 2009).

3.2.1 Challenges in Defining Multicultural People

A recurring challenge in the study of Multicultural people is defining who is considered Multicultural, and how that is assessed (Nguyen & Benet-Martínez, 2007). Multiculturalism has been defined based on demographic and/or psychological criteria, such as having exposure to multiple cultural groups through a history of immigration and/or self-identifying as Multicultural (Nguyen & Benet-Martínez, 2007). Multiculturalism is also a strategy of acculturation that incorporates both the heritage culture and the mainstream culture through multiple dimensions including values, practices, and identification (Schwartz et al., 2010).

Moreover, although as much as 94 percent of research on acculturation uses correlational methods, acculturation could be considered a causal hypothesis, testing how exposure to a second culture leads to changes in people's cultural identities and well-being (Bierwiaczonek & Kunst, 2021; Nguyen & Benet-Martínez, 2013; Redfield et al., 1936; though see Grigoryev & Berry, 2021 for an argument that acculturation is a structural framework rather than a causal one). A minority of studies in a recent meta-analysis were longitudinal (approximately 10 percent of studies) or experimental (approximately 3 percent of studies) and therefore better suited to test causality (Bierwiaczonek & Kunst, 2021; Kunst, 2021). The longitudinal studies demonstrated weak evidence of a positive association between an integration acculturation style and sociocultural adaptation, even though methodological restraints on the meta-analysis may have overestimated the effect size (Bierwiaczonek & Kunst, 2021). Future work should validate experimental paradigms manipulating participants' acculturation (Kunst, 2021).

Despite these conceptual debates and methodological critiques, much research has focused on integration as a specific way to acculturate. Six meta-analyses have examined the association between integration and well-being, demonstrating generally weak positive associations (Berry et al., 2022; Bierwiaczonek & Kunst, 2021; Kunst, 2021; Nguyen & Benet-Martínez, 2013; Stogianni et al., 2021; Yoon et al., 2013). Moreover, these have demonstrated high heterogeneity between studies, indicating moderator variables may play a key role in this relationship (Kunst, 2021). For example, whether migration is voluntary or involuntary has been found to be an important moderator of the association between acculturation and well-being (Schwartz et al., 2010).

Further, frame switching is a commonly used paradigm to study Multicultural people's cognitive access to cultural schemas. Participants are primed with cultural icons of each of their cultural backgrounds (e.g., an American flag for mainstream US culture, and a Chinese dragon for Chinese culture) to measure the role of culture in the types of causal attributions Multicultural people make for a target's behavior, identification, independent and interdependent self-construal, self-stereotyping, attitudes, ingroup favoritism, emotional expression, and neural representations of the self and others (Cheng et al., 2021; De Leersnyder, 2017; Hong et al., 2000; Ng et al., 2010; Sui et al., 2007; Verkuyten & Pouliasi, 2006). This switching can be moderated by how integrated participants' cultural identities are, such that people whose identities are more integrated respond congruently to cultural primes, whereas participants whose identities are less integrated respond incongruently to cultural primes (Cheng et al., 2006).

Another challenge in research with Multicultural populations is establishing measurement invariance. Measurement invariance is a psychometric standard that ensures a measure is conceptually similar across different populations. Among Multicultural populations, this can include different groups of Multicultural Americans (e.g., Asian Americans and Latinx Americans), different generational groups, and Multicultural people who speak different languages (Guo et al., 2009; Schwartz, Vignoles, et al., 2014). Establishing measurement invariance is necessary to draw conclusions about cultural differences because measures must be conceptually similar across groups to be comparable. Measurement invariance is met when a questionnaire holds the same structure and meaning across groups, suggesting that any differences found between groups reflect true differences in the construct, rather than differences in how groups understood the questionnaire. Research with Multicultural populations has centered this requirement across various research questions, including measures of acculturation, multicultural involvement, and family functioning (Cano et al., 2016; Guo et al., 2009; Schwartz, Benet-Martínez, et al., 2014). For example, the Bicultural Involvement Questionnaire – Short Version was invariant across generational status, indicating that differences found between generational groups were unlikely to be due to differences in how participants interpreted the questions (Guo et al., 2009).

3.3 Comparing Methodological Approaches

Across both Multiracial and Multicultural populations, researchers have faced a challenge in defining who is considered a member of these groups. Across both bodies of work, inclusion criteria are often inconsistent between studies, making it difficult to draw broad, generalizable conclusions. For example, researchers disagree on whether to consider Latinx a separate racial group, and thereby consider people who have Latinx and another racial background as Multiracial. The socially constructed nature of race makes these determinations dynamic and fluid (Song, 2021). The US census considers Latinx an ethnicity, so people who select a racial identity and Latinx ethnicity are not counted among the "Two or More" Multiracial population. However, there is evidence that Latinx populations themselves consider Latinx a racial group, with as many as 18.5 million people selecting "Some Other Race" and writing in "Latino" or "Hispanic" in the 2010 US census (Gonzalez-Barrera & Lopez, 2015; Herman, 2020; Hitlin et al., 2007). Thus, people with multiple racial backgrounds where one is Latinx may consider themselves Multiracial but would not be considered such by the US census and some researchers (e.g., Amaro & Zambrana, 2000; Doyle & Kao, 2007; Udry et al., 2003). Because the multiracial literature is also inconsistent in its inclusion of Latinx people as Multiracial, it is difficult to know whether findings may be expected to generalize to Multiracial people with Latinx heritage.

Similarly, Latinx Americans are highly represented in studies on the association between multiculturalism and adjustment (Nguyen & Benet-Martínez, 2013), but how multiculturalism was defined within this population varies (Safa & Umaña-Taylor, 2021). For example, multiculturalism among Latinx Americans has been operationalized as dual-cultural adaptation (e.g., integrating cultural practices, values, and identifications from both cultures; Berry, 1974), dual-cultural identity (e.g., measuring processes through which cultural identities are formed and maintained), Bicultural identity integration, and Bicultural competence (Safa & Umaña-Taylor, 2021). Thus, whether Latinx Americans would be considered Multiracial, Multicultural, or both, is conceptually unclear based on current definitions of being Latinx. Therefore, future research would benefit from clearer and more justified inclusion criteria to properly test for generalizability of multiracial findings for those with Latinx heritage.

There are some similarities in the topics studied across both populations. For example, a large body of work is dedicated to understanding identity development of both Multiracial and Multicultural populations. Both approaches focus on correlates between these identities and well-being. Here, the literatures share similar limitations in the lack of experimental tests and future research would benefit from greater use of longitudinal and experimental methods to address the directionality of this relationship (Bierwiaczonek & Kunst, 2021). Moreover, while multicultural research often tests measurement invariance when making comparisons across subpopulations, research with Multiracial populations would benefit from including this psychometric test in relevant studies more often.

There are also differences in each field's approach to the study of identity. Multiracial research focuses both on understanding people's identity development, as well as how they are categorized by others (e.g., Ho et al., 2020). As a result, there is also an emphasis on phenotypic presentation within this work. In contrast, multicultural research is dominated by an acculturation perspective that highlights identity integration as an acculturation strategy and identity endorsed by Multicultural people (e.g., Nguyen & Benet-Martínez, 2013). While some work also examines how Multicultural people are perceived and categorized by others (e.g., Kosic & Phalet, 2006; Kunst et al., 2018), theory and empirical findings are further developed in research among Multiracial people. Open questions remain surrounding how phenotypic presentation influences categorization of Multicultural people and their own identity development processes. For example, are Multicultural people categorized according to hypodescent? How are cultural and racial hierarchies used when categorizing a Multicultural person? Similarly, the construct of acculturation has scarcely been applied to Multiracial populations, although it could be argued that Multiracial people have sustained contact with two racial groups through socialization (Liu et al., 2019). Does an integrated racial identity convey similar benefits for Multiracial people as for Multicultural people?

4 Socialization

Children learn about their racial and cultural background(s) through socialization from parents or other socializing agents such as other caregivers, teachers, peers, and media, and through overt messages or covert means (e.g., exposure to racial and cultural diversity, décor in the home, parents' behaviors toward racial or cultural outgroup members; Hughes et al., 2006). The terminology used in the literature varies, with "racial socialization" commonly used in studies of monoracial and Black/White Multiracial families, while "ethnic socialization" or "cultural socialization" are commonly used in studies of Multiracial or Multicultural Asian and Latinx families (Atkin & Yoo, 2019; Hughes et al., 2006). For clarity, here we use *racial socialization* to describe the multidimensional process of learning about race across all multiracial backgrounds, and *ethnic socialization* to describe the multidimensional process of learning about culture across all multicultural backgrounds.

4.1 Multiracial Socialization

Racial socialization describes the multidimensional process through which children learn about race, identity, and discrimination (Atkin & Yoo, 2019). *Cultural socialization, promotion of mistrust, preparation for bias,* and *egalitarianism* are the most studied types of socialization among monoracial minority group members (Hughes et al., 2006). Racial socialization includes cultural socialization, or teaching children the cultural practices and customs of their racial group. Promotion of mistrust encourages children to be cautious around racial outgroup members, while preparation for bias describes teaching children about inequality and preparing them to deal with discrimination. Finally, egalitarianism promotes equality between racial groups and intergroup friendships (Hughes et al., 2006). Racial socialization is associated with various outcomes, including racial identity, quality of interpersonal relationships, self-esteem, academic achievement, psychological health, and behavioral adjustment (see Hughes et al., 2006; Huguley et al., 2019; Umaña-Taylor & Hill, 2020; Wang, Henry et al., 2020; Wang, Smith et al., 2020 for reviews). However, because most of this research has been conducted with minoritized monoracial families, racial socialization among Multiracial families is less understood (see Priest et al., 2014 for a review).

The existing findings among monoracial families are unlikely to generalize to Multiracial families, where children may be socialized to multiple racial groups, and may not share a racial identity with their parents (Atkin & Yoo, 2019). For example, a Multiracial Asian/Latinx child would have an Asian and a Latinx parent, neither of whom would have the lived experience of growing up as a Multiracial child. Parents in interracial relationships have reported sadness and concern with the potential loss of cultural knowledge between generations and a lack of phenotypic connection to extended family (Song & Gutierrez, 2015; Wu et al., 2020). Previous work on the racial socialization practices of parents of monoracial children has not demonstrated similar concerns, indicating this may be a unique aspect of Multiracial socialization.

As described earlier, Multiracial identity development models were historically a focus of multiracial research, and some of these models explicitly attended to socialization processes (e.g., Collins, 2000; Jacobs, 1992; Kerwin et al., 1993; Kich, 1992; Poston, 1990; Wijeyesinghe, 2001; Williams, 1999). For example, Wijeyesinghe's (2001) Factor Model of Multiracial Identity Development and Root's (2003) Ecological Framework for Understanding Multiracial Identity Development include socialization as a predictor of identity development. A recent review of twenty-one articles studying Multiracial racial socialization found most studies (fourteen) were qualitative, and many (nine) included Black/White participants. These studies focused largely on cultural and egalitarian socialization, and often applied monoracial frames to the Multiracial population (Atkin & Yoo, 2019). However, racial socialization, as it has been typically conceptualized and studied among monoracial families, may relate to identity development differently for Multiracial families. For example, racial socialization was associated with greater identity exploration, but not with identity affirmation among Multiracial families (Brittian et al., 2013).

Indeed, Atkin and Yoo (2019) identified research on other dimensions of racial socialization specific to Multiracial families, including identity socialization, negative socialization, exposure to diversity, and no socialization. A meta-ethnographic review of qualitative research on Black/White Multiracial socialization identified three themes overlapping with the Atkin and Yoo (2019) findings, including messages about monoracial Black people, color-evasiveness (i.e., avoiding discussing race and being racially categorized), and messages about multiracial experiences (e.g., encouraging pride in being Multiracial and preparing children for both bias and privilege they may experience due to their background; Stokes et al., 2021).

Identity socialization describes messages family members transmit about how Multiracial people should identify (Atkin & Yoo, 2019). For example, identity socialization was often seen through family members encouraging their Multiracial child to identify with their racial minority background, following the norms of hypodescent (Chancler et al., 2017; Jackson et al., 2019; O'Donoghue, 2005), though others, particularly if they did not have Black ancestry, were encouraged to identify as White (King, 2013). Socialization as monoracial Black often includes both messages to prepare children for bias, and teaching affirmative racial group practices (Stokes et al., 2021). Other families reported encouraging their child to identify as Biracial, either directly by providing them this label, or indirectly (Rauktis et al., 2016; Stone & Dolbin-MacNab, 2017; Stokes et al., 2021). Some parents report researching best socialization practices for Biracial children and teaching their child to be proud that they are mixed (Stone & Dolbin-MacNab, 2017). Caregivers sometimes demonstrated cultural humility, wherein they supported their child's autonomy in selecting their own identity (Franco & McElroy-Heltzel, 2019). Which of these different approaches is taken may depend on ecological factors, such as how salient race is in the family's social context (Stokes et al., 2021).

Those families who engaged in negative socialization encouraged their child to avoid or mistrust racial groups, even those racial groups that comprise the child's ancestry (Harris et al., 2013). For example, one sample of Multiracial emerging adults recalled feeling disconnected from their parents in their childhood because of a lack of communication surrounding race, identity, and discrimination (Atkin & Jackson, 2021). In contrast, some Multiracial families intentionally try to expose their child to diversity by living in a Multiracial community in order to fill socialization gaps that parents themselves may not be able to do (O'Donoghue, 2005; Snyder, 2012). Living in diverse communities can provide role models and teach children about experiences their parents may not have themselves, such as White parents who may not experience the racism their child is exposed to. Other work demonstrates interracial contact may be a significant event that catalyzes socialization and identity development (Cardwell et al., 2020). Finally, some research has demonstrated that Multiracial families may opt out of racial socialization by failing to discuss race at all, avoiding the topic whenever it comes up (Jackson et al., 2019; King, 2013; Snyder, 2012). This may lead to less closeness between parents, and some emerging adults report resentment at not having learned more about their racial backgrounds (Stokes et al., 2021). Though nascent, this existing literature demonstrates how Multiracial socialization shares commonalities with traditional studies of monoracial socialization, and also requires specific attention to the socialization of multiple racial identities.

Very few studies have directly compared Multiracial and monoracial socialization. Among a sample of caregivers drawn from five regions of the US, caregivers of Multiracial children reported similar levels of cultural socialization as caregivers of Asian, Black, and White children, and higher cultural socialization than caregivers of Latinx children (Albuja et al., 2022). Caregivers of Multiracial children also reported similar levels of preparation for bias as caregivers of Asian, White, Black, and Latinx children. Finally, caregivers of Multiracial children reported similar levels of egalitarian socialization as caregivers of Black, Latinx, and White children, and higher egalitarian socialization than caregivers of Asian children (Albuja et al., 2022). Though there may be some differences, in general, these findings demonstrate similar overall amounts of socialization between Multiracial and monoracial families when socialization is not measured using multiracial-specific scales.

4.2 Multicultural Socialization

Research on ethnic socialization often includes Multicultural populations as defined here, without necessarily using the term "Multicultural." For example, ethnic socialization stemmed from research with immigrant Asian and Latinx populations, and studied how families socialized their children to both mainstream American culture and their heritage culture (Knight et al., 1993a,; Knight et al., 1993b; Ou & McAdoo, 1993; Quintana & Vera, 1999).

Thus, there is conceptual overlap in ethnic and racial socialization, and both are conceptualized to include cultural socialization, preparation for bias, promotion of mistrust, and egalitarianism (Hughes et al., 2006). Moreover, ethnic socialization is associated with similar outcomes as racial socialization, including ethnic identity, academic achievement, and well-being (see Ayón et al., 2020; Hughes et al., 2006; Huguley et al., 2019; Umaña-Taylor & Hill, 2020; Wang, Henry et al., 2020; Wang, Smith et al., 2020 for reviews).

For Multicultural families, socialization represents an attempt to pass on the heritage culture in the face of pressures to assimilate to mainstream US culture (Hughes et al., 2006; Knight et al., 2011; Mchitarjan & Reisenzein, 2015; Umaña-Taylor et al., 2009). Indeed, parents' lower assimilation to mainstream US culture is associated with greater ethnic socialization to the heritage culture (Knight et al., 1993b; Quintana & Vera, 1999). Similarly, earlier generational immigrants socialize their children to their heritage culture, and discuss discrimination more than later generational immigrants, because they have more first-hand experience with the heritage culture than later generational immigrants (Knight et al., 2011; Umaña-Taylor et al., 2009; Umaña-Taylor et al., 2014). Yet, aspects of ethnic socialization such as family gatherings, traditional meals, and Spanish language use were found to be shared across different generations of Mexican American and Puerto Rican mothers (Umaña-Taylor & Yazedjian, 2006).

Specifically, ethnic socialization involves the transmission of cultural values (Knight et al., 2011). For example, Mexican American parents' cultural values of respect, obligation, reference, religion, and support were associated with greater ethnic socialization, and ultimately greater adoption of these values by Mexican American adolescents (Knight et al., 2011). Similarly, Mexican American parents passed on their familism values, which prioritize family ties and obligations, to their adolescents (Calderón et al., 2011; Knight et al., 2016; Kulish et al., 2019). Among Chinese American parents, shame, modesty, and filial piety (i.e., a value that intersects with face and harmony) are passed onto children through ethnic socialization (Lieber et al., 2004; Luo et al., 2013). Ethnic socialization can also include sociopolitical discussions that socialize youth to civic engagement (Carranza, 2007; Pinetta et al., 2020) and documentation status socialization that orients youth to the causes and consequences of their legal immigration status in the US (Ayón, 2016; Cross et al., 2021). Finally, socialization among Multicultural families can also involve teaching children a heritage language or traveling to a parent's home country (Ayón et al., 2020; though see Villalobo Solís [2021] for evidence that visits to Puerto Rico constitute a construct separate from ethnic socialization).

Multicultural parents not only seek to pass on traditional values and beliefs from their heritage culture, but also socialize their child to be successful in the US through "American" ways (Aldoney & Cabrera 2016; Cheah et al. 2013; John & Montgomery, 2012; Lieber et al. 2004; Uttal & Han, 2011). For example, Chinese mothers' cultural orientation toward Chinese-American culture (rather than toward Chinese culture or American culture, respectively) was associated with higher Multicultural socialization beliefs, and with adolescents' Chinese-American cultural orientation (Kim & Hou, 2016). However, Chinese mothers' cultural orientation toward Chinese or American cultures was not related to adolescents' Chinese or American cultural orientation, demonstrating that Multicultural socialization may be transmitted intergenerationally when parents are high in Multicultural socialization beliefs (Kim & Hou, 2016). Similarly, Multicultural adolescents of various backgrounds reported receiving cultural socialization to both their heritage culture and the mainstream culture (Wang et al., 2015).

Other work has examined parents' socialization goals for their Multicultural children, or their ideal for their children's cultural orientations that would most help them have healthy and successful lives (John & Montgomery, 2012). For Indian American families, these goals may vary in the extent to which they are autonomy versus family-centered, promote a Multicultural versus an ethnic identity, and encourage academic achievement versus social competence (John & Montgomery, 2012). One study found that parents may take a blended approach, where their socialization goals include both values of the heritage culture and mainstream American values, or a traditional approach that prioritizes cultural continuity through family-centered and ethnic identity goals (John & Montgomery, 2012). Similarly, Mexican American families included both heritage cultural values of *respeto* and more mainstream cultural values of independence in their socialization of their adolescents (Kim et al., 2019). Finally, recent theoretical developments propose a developmental approach to understanding how Multicultural people negotiate their two identities. For example, people may negotiate their identities through exploration, alternating, integration, and hybridizing (Meca et al., 2019). The use of these strategies is influenced by the familial cultural context, including parents' socialization toward each cultural orientation (Meca et al., 2019; Umaña-Taylor et al., 2006).

4.3 Comparing Multiracial and Multicultural Socialization

Racial and ethnic socialization share a theoretical foundation primarily grounded in a bioecological model of child development that emphasizes children's socialization within the microsystem of the family, as well as within broader societal and structural factors (Bronfenbrenner & Morris, 2006; Titzmann & Lee, 2018). Following, many constructs overlap, including the cultural socialization, preparation for bias, egalitarianism, and promotion of mistrust dimensions of both racial and ethnic socialization (Hughes et al., 2006). However, several other dimensions of socialization have been added to the study of ethnic socialization, including familism and documentation socialization among Latinx Multicultural families (Ayón, 2016; Cross et al., 2021; Kulish et al., 2019), and filial piety among Chinese Multicultural families (Lieber et al., 2004; Luo et al., 2013). These dimensions have not been studied among families with Multiracial children. In contrast, racial socialization of Multiracial children has expanded to also include identity socialization, negative socialization, exposure to diversity, and no socialization (Atkin & Yoo, 2019). These dimensions have not been studied among Multicultural families. Thus, while racial and ethnic socialization share many theoretical foundations, each has been expanded to include dimensions of socialization more specific to each population.

Moreover, parents and families are often studied as the principal socializing agents within both populations (Brittian et al., 2013; Chancler et al., 2017; Knight et al., 2011). Specifically, cultural socialization most often focuses on mothers as the socializing agents (Knight et al. 2011; Su & Costigan, 2009). For example, the family obligation expectations of Chinese mothers in Canada were related to children's ethnic identity development, while fathers' expectations were not (Su & Costigan, 2009). However, other work demonstrates that fathers' role may be more substantive than mothers' in cultural socialization toward mainstream American culture (Paquette, 2004; Zeiders et al. 2015). Yet, other work has failed to find caregiver gender differences in cultural socialization of adolescents (Kim & Hou, 2016). Grandparents also have a critical role, as they may promote multiracial and multicultural pride, or may serve as monocentric gatekeepers who deny Multiracial and Multicultural identities and limit identification with a monoracial or monocultural group by gatekeeping behaviors such as language (Jackson et al., 2020). Future research should expand study on socialization from grandparents and other agents, especially because each socialization agent may pass on their racial or cultural background. Thus, in studies of Multiracial and Multicultural children, it is especially important to study how socialization from both parents or other caregivers interact to influence children's identities. Relatedly, much research has focused on adolescence as a time of identity development, though research with Multicultural populations also accounts for the developmental period when participants immigrated to the US (Hong & Schmidt, 2021). This suggests there may be developmental differences in socialization time periods between Multiracial and Multicultural children that have not been studied.

The dimensions of socialization specific to Multiracial children focus on Multiracial identification and interracial intergroup relations, such as through negative socialization that encourages mistrust of other racial groups (Harris et al., 2013). In contrast, the dimensions of socialization specific to Multicultural children focus on value transmission and issues surrounding immigration (Ayón, 2016). While theoretical models of both racial and ethnic identity development include socialization as an important mechanism for identity development (Umaña-Taylor & Fine, 2004; Wijeyesinghe, 2001), to date there is less research on socialization to the Multicultural identity label compared to the Multiracial identity label (Atkin & Yoo, 2019). Indeed, research on cultural identity often studies people's identification with their ethnic identity (e.g., Latinx American or Asian American) rather than with a "Multicultural" identity (e.g., Gartner et al., 2014). This likely stems from conceptual and methodological overlap between racial and ethnic identity that has prompted the use of similar measures among monoracial and Multicultural populations (Umaña-Taylor et al., 2014). Open questions remain surrounding what demographic, contextual, and psychological variables influence people's identification with a pan-ethnic label of "Multicultural." This has important implications for coalition-building across Multicultural people with different cultural backgrounds.

5 Identity Negotiation

Social identities are negotiated within different contexts (Deaux & Ethier, 1998; Roccas & Brewer, 2002). Negotiating a social identity describes the process through which identities are created and cocreated in relation to others in a dynamic process (Yep, 2002). Indeed, social identity theory outlines how the context can influence the salience of a specific identity, hypothesizing that increased salience leads to increased identification (Haslam et al., 1992). Identity negotiation is an especially salient aspect of the multiracial and multicultural experience because racial and cultural identity can be flexible, fluid, and context-dependent (Lou et al., 2011; Sanchez & Garcia, 2009; Sanchez et al., 2009; Wilton et al., 2013). Moreover, static Multiracial and Multicultural identities may also be achieved through the process of identity negotiation. Previous research has identified Multiracial and Multicultural people's negotiation strategies, including processes of integrating their identities. Moreover, this work has demonstrated how people negotiate their identities through interactions with others, and the well-being consequences of these negotiation strategies.

5.1 Multiracial Identity Negotiation

5.1.1 Identity Negotiation Strategies

Several models describe identity negotiation strategies Multiracial people may use. As described earlier, Rockquemore (1999) outlined a taxonomy for Black-White Multiracial people, including singular, border, protean, and transcendent identities. Estimates of protean identity among Multiracial adults range from 4.8 percent to 30 percent, meaning they sometimes identify with one group and at other times identify with another group (Lou et al., 2011; Lusk et al., 2010; Rockquemore & Brunsma, 2002).

Similarly, Roccas and Brewer (2002) outlined four strategies people may use to manage social identities, including but extending beyond multiple racial identities. These strategies include (1) intersection (identifying only with the intersection of multiple groups, such as an Asian/White Multiracial person viewing only other Asian/White Multiracial people as ingroup members), (2) dominance (identifying with only one social group), (3) compartmentalization (identifying with each of the two groups in different settings), and (4) merger (identifying with both groups simultaneously). Additional research has applied a framework of identity integration from studies of Multicultural people to Multiracial people. This work describes racial distance as the perceived separation between one's racial identities, and racial conflict as the perceived incompatibility between one's racial identities (Cheng & Lee, 2009). Identity integration can be experimentally shifted, and influenced by experiences of discrimination. For example, after recalling positive experiences related to being Multiracial, participants reported lower racial distance and conflict compared to baseline (Cheng & Lee, 2009). In contrast, greater experiences of discrimination are associated with higher racial conflict (Jackson et al., 2012) and distance (Reid Marks et al., 2020).

5.1.2 Identity Negotiation through Social Interactions

Multiracial identity is partly negotiated through interactions with others. This can involve feedback from others about how much a Multiracial person is conforming to group norms and behavioral expectations (Orbe et al., 2015). For example, Multiracial participants in a qualitative study described being told they act or talk "White" (Orbe et al., 2015). Similarly, Black/White Multiracial adults have described identifying as Black because this reflects how others perceive and treat them (Khanna, 2010). Multiracial identity is also influenced by the racial composition and identity threats in an environment. Indeed, Multiracial people identified less as White and perceived greater threat to their White identity when they were in the presence of more people who shared their racial minority background (Wilton et al., 2013). Relatedly, how Multiracial people negotiate their identities may be influenced by the context. For example, 75 percent of adolescents who identified as Multiracial at home did not identify as Multiracial at school (Harris & Sim, 2002). This study demonstrates how for Multiracial people, negotiating racial identity involves both internal identifications as well as responding to others' perceptions and other influences of the social environment. Moreover, Multiracial people's identity can also change throughout the life course. For example, in one estimate, 30 percent of Multiracial adults reported changing their identity throughout their life (Pew Research Center, 2015b).

5.1.3 Well-Being Consequences of Identity Negotiation

This fluidity has implications for Multiracial people's well-being and belonging consequences. Multiracial people who reported identifying with different racial groups in different contexts also reported greater depressive symptoms (Sanchez et al., 2009). However, this association may be weaker among people who have a higher dialectical self-view, meaning they have a greater tolerance for contradictions within themselves (Sanchez et al., 2009). By nature of being fluid and dynamic, Multiracial people report viewing race as more socially constructed than monoracial people (Shih et al., 2007). This perspective buffered Multiracial people from negative stereotype threat effects (Shih et al., 2007). Other research has studied monoracial perceiver's responses to such identity fluidity. White participants viewed Multiracial targets who changed their racial presentation in response to a situation as untrustworthy and unlikable, a response that was mediated by explicit stereotyping of Multiracial people as confused about their identity (Albuja et al., 2018). Relatedly, monoracial Asian perceivers expected Asian/White Multiracial people to identify as White in instances of anti-Asian discrimination, which was associated with Asians' distrust of Asian/White Multiracial people (Chen et al., 2019).

5.2 Multicultural Identity Negotiation

Initial investigations focused on the acculturation strategies of immigrants in order to categorize Multicultural people into "types." As described earlier, Berry's (1980) highly influential acculturation model provided four categories that Multicultural people fall into, depending on how strongly and actively connected they are to their heritage (i.e., minority) culture and to the main-stream (i.e., majority) culture: integration, assimilation, separation, and mar-ginalization (Berry, 1980; Berry et al., 2006). These initial four categories formed the basis for additional "microcategories" that endeavored to further differentiate the experiences of Multicultural individuals within these four types. The greatest attention was given to the integration category, but LaFromboise and colleagues (1993) provided distinctions between Multicultural individuals who alternated between their contextually bound identities (later inspiring work on frame switching), versus those who embraced a stable multicultural strategy by identifying simultaneously with their two independent cultures, versus those who adopted a fusion strategy leading to a singular hybridized culture. Thus, how a Multicultural person maintains both cultures manifests differently between Multicultural individuals and for each individual over time and context. Here, we review multicultural subcategories and subsequent negotiation processes that have been identified within those individuals who identify with all their cultures.

5.2.1 Integration

The identity configuration that has received the most empirical attention has been integration, particularly as conceived by Benet-Martínez and colleagues (see Section 2.4.2). Identity integration is dependent on each Multicultural individual's own subjective perceptions of their cultures' similarity and com-patibility. Given that it is based on perceptions, identity integration is subject to change as a Multicultural person continues to experience their cultures and the attitudes of others in their cultural groups. Further, the cognitive-developmental model of social identity integration (Amiot et al., 2007; Yampolsky et al., 2013, 2016) and the transformative theory of biculturalism (West et al., 2017) both underscore the cognitive effort required to actively reconcile one's cultural groups and identities by resolving the conflicts and discrepancies between them, as well as by appreciating the larger-scale cohesion that exists between these entities (Amiot et al., 2007; Tadmor & Tetlock, 2006). There are several strategies or routes to integrating, such as valuing the differing perspectives of each of one's cultural groups as equally valid and beneficial (Tadmor & Tetlock, 2006; Tadmor et al., 2009) and viewing one's cultural backgrounds as comple-mentary rather than contradictory (Amiot et al., 2007; Yampolsky et al., 2013, 2016). It is through this active integrating work that one achieves an overall harmony between these distinct parts of oneself (Benet-Martínez & Haritatos, 2005). The literature on Multicultural people's integration of cultural identities has thus far demonstrated that greater integration predicts greater narrative coherence and self-esteem (Yampolsky et al., 2013, 2016), greater creativity in novel uses tasks, and greater reported professional success, such as employee promotions (Tadmor et al., 2009; Tadmor, Galinsky, et al., 2012). These findings largely support that integrating cultural identities produces unique and adaptive outcomes for managing multiple cultural identities.

5.2.2 Alternation and Frame Switching

Faced with the demands of different cultural contexts, many Multicultural individuals can come to see their identities as compartmentalized – independently bound to each cultural context, resulting in an alternating strategy by which a Multicultural person only identifies with one culture at a time. Relatedly but not necessarily tied, is their ability to frame switch, by which a Multicultural person adapts aspects of cognition and behavior to fit each culture's norms. Qualitative studies show that Multicultural people are often aware that they adapt themselves to their cultural environments, and many do so intentionally (Yampolsky et al., 2013). Recognition of frame switching may lead some Multicultural people to experience compartmentalization or alternation, the experience of keeping one's cultural identities separate and context-specific (Yampolsky et al., 2016; also see, Downie et al., 2006). However, there is debate over the extent to which frame switching and alternating identities are bound versus independent, with some researchers pointing to instances of highly integrated Multicultural people still frame switching and the moderating role of identity integration and authenticity on the relative positive versus negative outcomes of frame switching (Firat & Noels, 2021; Hong & Schmidt, 2021; Meca et al., 2019; Szabó et al., 2020; Ward et al., 2021).

5.2.3 Hybridization

Another negotiation strategy is hybridization, or combining cultures into a new form that is distinct from its precursor cultures (Doucerain et al., 2013; Zhang et al., 2014). A common result is the emergence of a third culture that bridges the source cultures. For instance, Jewish and Asian Americans have reported that embracing both individualism and collectivism increased one's obligation to the larger society (Oyserman et al., 1998), which can be seen as a presumably more adaptive solution, particularly when living in a complex, multicultural context. Moreover, hybridizing may lead Multicultural people toward not only changes in self-concept, but also greater cognitive complexity. Since hybridizing involves borrowing aspects of different cultures and transmuting them into new forms, it may help Multicultural people bridge knowledge from diverse perspectives and recombine ideas into novel solutions. For example, compared with less blended Asian Americans, those who were more blended generated more creative dishes when given both Asian and American ingredients (Cheng et al., 2008) and showed increased creativity on a culture-neutral unusual uses test after being primed with both cultures versus a single culture (Saad et al., 2013).

5.3 Comparing Identity Negotiation

A review of the identity negotiation research with Multiracial and Multicultural people reveals many commonalities. In both cases, initial investigations were primarily concerned with creating types according to people's relative strengths of identification with each of their racial or cultural groups (e.g., Berry, 1980; Roccas & Brewer, 2002). There are some common themes in the overlap between the categories created within the different typological models. For instance, a cluster of categories represent people who feel torn between their groups, perceiving those groups to conflict with one another and be mutually exclusive, as reflected by the protean Multiracial individual and the compartmentalized or alternating Multicultural individual (LaFromboise et al., 1993; Rockquemore, 1999; Ward et al., 2018). On the other hand, the border Multiracial and integrated Multicultural (Amiot et al., 2007; Rockquemore, 1999) categories include individuals who bridge their groups, finding shared elements and seeing harmony or complements in the differences. If these border and integrated strategies are akin to bridge building between two lands, the merger Multiracial and hybridizing Multicultural (Roccas & Brewer, 2002; West et al., 2017; Zhang et al., 2014) strategies instead entail creating a new island between two lands – the individual holds a single identity that reflects the idiosyncratic way they have combined elements of their two groups.

Importantly, a person's negotiation strategies are most often unfixed, varying across their lifespan as well as moment to moment in response to external pressures and support. Social interactions with friends, family, and society at large powerfully shape and constrain Multiracial and Multicultural identities, whether through historical or ongoing conflict between their groups or more general messaging that a person can or cannot fully belong to more than one group (West et al., 2021; Yampolsky et al., 2021). For example, discrimination experiences push individuals in both populations toward more fractured identities and can thwart efforts to integrate and find stability in their dual identities (Yampolsky et al., 2015; 2020). A pressing challenge in modern ever-diversifying societies will be to identify and ameliorate the barriers Multiracial and Multicultural people face in their identity journeys. Future research would benefit from understanding how supportive environments that promote identity autonomy and exploration influence identity negotiation strategies as one pathway to support Multiracial and Multicultural people's well-being.

In both literatures, we also see increased microcategorizing of Multiracial and Multicultural people as the dominant trend until only recently. A budding new perspective in both fields moves away from labeling individuals according to categories and instead reconceptualizes the strategies that underlie the prior categories as skills that a person can develop and draw on flexibly as they negotiate their changing social relationships and attitudes (Hong, 2013; West et al., 2017). One promise of this new approach is the potential to pinpoint the mechanisms through which being Multiracial or Multicultural affects a person's characteristics and abilities. For instance, both multiraciality and multicultural-ism have been repeatedly linked to greater cognitive flexibility, but the precise reason for these effects is less clear. In considering the range of identity configurations as processes that individuals use to negotiate their groups, new research can investigate what exactly individuals are doing that fosters their flexible thinking. As examples provided by West and colleagues (2017), does frame switching strengthen the more general executive functions of task switch-ing and inhibition? Might the extensive bridge-building work that makes integration possible transfer to greater dialecticism and wise reasoning, which are characterized by the ability to simultaneously consider opposing perspec-tives? Reframing prior work on identity categories as active processes – what Multiracial and Multicultural people *do* instead of what they *are* – holds potential to advance our understanding and methods around the causes and effects of being Multiracial or Multicultural (Sam & Ward, 2021).

Despite commonalities between multiracial and multicultural typologies, differences also emerge in the nuances of certain configurations. For example, the intersectional identity is a more specific, discrete classification of a Multiracial individual who only identifies with their exact combination of races (Roccas & Brewer, 2002) in a way that differs from Multicultural hybridization. Namely, the intersectional Multiracial identity can be thought of as multiplicative or interactive in nature where identity A is moderated or qualified by identity B, and intersectional identity AB can only be understood fully through their interaction. In contrast, a hybridized Multicultural identity is a personalized combination of aspects of identity A and identity B into a new identity AB that is rather removed from its two sources. Another category difference emerges in considering the strategy of focusing on super-ordinate identities rather than one's cultural or racial identities (Rockquemore, 1999; Yampolsky et al., 2016). It is unclear whether these differences reflect unexplored identity configurations that exist for each population, and/or if there may be important differences in the social construction of race and culture that lead to certain distinct identity choices and configurations. Extending research with both populations to include multiple other social identities, and account for the unique influence of the social context, would help researchers understand the complexity of identity negotiation more comprehensively.

6 Discrimination

US society is organized by a racial hierarchy that places White people above all other racial groups, and a cultural hierarchy that places "Americanness" above "foreignness" (Roberts & Rizzo, 2020; Zou & Cheryan, 2017). Multiracial populations, like other racially minoritized populations, are subordinated within the existing racial hierarchy. Similarly, Multicultural populations are often seen as foreign or not fully American (Devos & Banaji, 2005). As a result, both Multiracial and Multicultural populations experience interpersonal and structural discrimination. Discrimination may occur in different forms, and is often associated with negative relational and well-being outcomes (Araújo Dawson, 2009; Christophe et al., 2021; Franco et al., 2021a; Gee et al., 2007, 2009; Jang et al., 2010; Lee & Ahn, 2011; Miller et al., 2011; Norman & Chen, 2021; Salahuddin & O'Brien, 2011; Tran et al., 2010; Yoo et al., 2016).

6.1 Multiracial Discrimination

Multiracial populations are marginalized in various ways, including through monoracism, challenges to their identities, and microaggressions (Franco et al., 2021a). In fact, Multiracial college students report experiencing discrimination at higher rates than White, Latinx (Hurtado et al., 2015), and Black students (Brackett et al., 2006). Similarly, in a nationally representative study of US adults, Multiracial people reported experiencing greater discrimination than White and Asian adults, and lower discrimination than Black adults (Nalven et al., 2021). For Multiracial people, discrimination may be perpetrated by both White people and people of color (Rockquemore & Brunsma, 2007), though some evidence suggests Multiracial people may be rejected less by other Multiracial people than monoracial ingroup members (Norman et al., 2021). Moreover, the racism Multiracial people experience may target their minoritized identities, or their Multiracial identity (Salahuddin & O'Brien, 2011), and can be perpetrated by strangers as well as family members (Franco & Carter, 2019; Franco et al., 2021a; Nadal et al., 2011; Salahuddin & O'Brien, 2011).

6.1.1 Monoracism and Identity Challenges

Monoracism describes, "a social system of psychological inequality where individuals who do not fit monoracial categories may be oppressed on systemic and interpersonal levels because of underlying assumptions and beliefs in singular, discrete racial categories" (Johnston & Nadal, 2010, p. 125). This can manifest in several ways, including institutionally, such as through campus centers and faculty of color groups focused only on monoracial identities, or through demographic forms forcing people to choose only one identity (Hamako, 2014; Harris, 2016, 2021). Interpersonally, Multiracial people may experience challenges to their identities because they do not fit monoracial norms, where their self-identification is denied or questioned by others (Albuja, Gaither, et al., 2019; Albuja et al., 2019a; Albuja et al., 2020; Franco et al., 2016; Sanchez, 2010; Vargas & Stainback, 2016). In one qualitative study, Multiracial people reported that identity denial occurred because of incongruence between phenotype or ancestry and racial identity, or between behavior and stereotypes (Franco et al., 2016). For Multiracial people with Black ancestry, such challenges were most likely to come from monoracial Black people and were most hurtful when they came from Black people compared to perpetrators of other racial backgrounds (Franco & Franco, 2016). Identities may also be challenged through behavioral and phenotype invalidation, which occur when people's behavior and phenotype, respectively, do not match a perceiver's expectations (Franco & O'Brien, 2018). More ambiguous challenges to identity, through questions such as, "What are you?" are more common than direct denial of one's identity (Albuja, et al., 2019a).

Though identity challenges seem to be a ubiquitous experience for Multiracial people, there is variation in how people respond to these challenges. For example, 22 percent of participants in a qualitative study reported resisting challenges to their identity through spoken disagreement, while 16 percent reported deflecting and not protesting (Franco et al., 2016). However, when Multiracial participants imagined their identities being questioned by others, most participants (71 percent) reported they would disclose their racial identity, while a smaller percentage reported they would correct the communicator (13 percent; Tran et al., 2016). Moreover, participants were more likely to report that they would end the conversation if the question came from a White person than if communicator race was unspecified (Tran et al., 2010).

6.1.2 Microaggressions

Multiracial people may also experience short, everyday negative communications related to being Multiracial, referred to as microaggressions (Harris,

2017a; Sue 2010). Johnston and Nadal (2010) created a taxonomy of multiracial microaggressions, which include exclusion, exoticization, assumption of a monoracial identity, denial of a multiracial reality, and pathologizing. Additional work has highlighted other multiracial microaggressions college students face, including being exoticized and pathologized as confused about their identity (Museus et al., 2016) or not being seen as monoracial enough to fit in (Harris, 2017a). These have also been reported by college student affairs professionals and faculty (Harris, 2017b, 2021). Among families, other researchers have noted microaggressions, including being isolated or favored within the family, authenticity being questioned, identity denial, and not learning about family backgrounds (Nadal et al., 2013). In addition, Multiracial people may also experience microaggressions shared by monoracial minoritized groups (Nadal et al., 2011). Such microaggressions may be less common for Multiracial people living in racially diverse contexts compared to homogenously White contexts (Meyers et al., 2020).

6.1.3 Identity-Related Stereotypes

Multiracial people may be stereotyped as confused about their identity, particularly when they demonstrated identity fluidity by identifying differently based on the context (Albuja et al., 2018). Similarly, Multiracial people may be stereotyped as socially unskilled, with implications for expected hiring decisions based on social skills during an interview (Remedios et al., 2012). Compared to monoracial Black and Asian college applicants, Multiracial Black/White and Asian/White applicants were judged to be less warm and less competent (Sanchez & Bonam, 2009). Across Multiracial backgrounds, perceivers expected Multiracial people to be attractive, but to not fit in (Skinner et al., 2020). Open questions remain surrounding how these stereotypes may be situationally activated and how they can guide behavior toward Multiracial people.

6.1.4 Monoracial Discrimination

Multiracial people have also described experiencing discrimination aimed at one of their monoracial ingroups, presumably because the perpetrator does not see them as Multiracial (Jackson, 2009). In other words, Multiracial people may be seen as monoracial and discriminated as such, rather than discriminated against for being Multiracial, as is described by monoracism. For instance, a Black/Latinx Multiracial person may be seen by others as Black and receive poor treatment, or be called a racial slur (Jackson, 2009). These experiences may be heavily influenced by phenotype and colorism, or a preference for lighter skin. Indeed, Black/Asian Multiracial people reported greater discrimination than Black/White Multiracial people (Root, 2001). Moreover, this discrimination may be identity incongruent if Multiracial people are perceived as and discriminated against as members of a monoracial group with which they do not identify (Franco et al., 2021b). These experiences are associated with greater depressive symptoms and with detaching from any racial identity (Franco & O'Brien, 2018; Franco et al., 2021b).

6.1.5 Well-Being Correlates of Discrimination

Discrimination has been found to be associated with several psychological well-being outcomes. For example, greater discrimination was associated with greater negative affect and distress symptoms, though this association was weaker for Multiracial people who reported a more integrated identity (Jackson et al., 2012). However, other research has demonstrated that identity integration mediates the association between Multiracial discrimination and depressive symptoms, such that greater discrimination is associated with lower identity integration, which in turn predicts greater depressive symptoms (Reid Marks et al., 2020). Similarly, identity denial has been associated with greater stress and depressive symptoms, as well as lower feelings of belonging, autonomy, and identity integration (Albuja, Gaither, et al., 2019; Albuja et al., 2019a; Sanchez, 2010; Townsend et al., 2009). Finally, greater discrimination, such as being picked on for not acting or looking like a racial group, being pressured to pick a race, and not being accepted by other racial groups, has also been associated with lower social connectedness and life satisfaction, as well as greater depressive symptoms, stress, anxiety, and negative affect (Christophe et al., 2021; Franco et al., 2021a; Norman & Chen, 2020; Salahuddin & O'Brien, 2011; Yoo et al., 2016). Discrimination has also been associated with greater substance use among Multiracial adults and adolescents, including heavy alcohol use (Choi et al., 2006; Nalven et al., 2021). This association may be especially strong when discrimination is perpetrated by family members (Franco & Carter, 2019). More recent research has noted the need to consider the association between discrimination and well-being within the ecological context. For example, discrimination and distress, negative affect, and life satisfaction were more weakly related in contexts where subjective racial diversity was high and Multiracial adults were able to create a third, multiracial space (Gabriel et al., 2021).

6.1.6 Identity and Social Network Correlates of Discrimination

Discrimination is also related to Multiracial people's identification and social connections. For example, more frequent discrimination was associated with greater self-stereotyping as Multiracial, perceiving Multiracial people as a more homogenous group, and greater solidarity with the Multiracial group (Giamo et al., 2012). In turn, greater self-stereotyping was associated with greater life satisfaction. Another study similarly found that, especially when perpetrated by White people, greater discrimination was associated with a stronger identification as Multiracial (Norman & Chen, 2020). Finally, among Multiracial youth, greater discrimination was associated with a stronger identification with their non-White background (Herman, 2004). These findings suggest Multiracial identity can be a protective factor against the negative consequences of discrimination.

Moreover, greater Multiracial discrimination was associated with feeling less accepted by White people and racial minority group members (Franco, 2019). Indeed, greater Multiracial discrimination was associated with reporting a lower proportion of White friends and greater proportion of Multiracial friends (Franco, 2019). In contrast, another study found that more frequent Multiracial discrimination was associated with creating a multiracial-specific space, but there was no relationship to the number of Multiracial friends reported (Yoo et al., 2016). Finally, Multiracial discrimination was associated with a greater desire to socialize with other Multiracial people (Miville et al., 2005; Museus et al., 2016).

6.2 Multicultural Discrimination

In the US, widespread associations equating American and White often lead to the perception that Multicultural Americans are not fully American (Devos & Banaji, 2005; Devos & Ma, 2008; Devos et al., 2010). As a result, Multicultural people can experience both interpersonal and structural discrimination (Araújo & Borrell, 2006; Miller et al., 2011, 2012). Interpersonal discrimination can include social exclusion, stigmatization, and physical or verbal harassment (Contrada et al., 2001; Zhao & Biernat, 2017), while structural discrimination can include anti-immigration policies, profiling by police, and a sociopolitical environment hostile to immigrants (Ayón & Becerra, 2013; Perreira & Pedroza, 2019). Multicultural populations report high levels of discrimination. For example, between 30 percent and 79.5 percent of Multicultural Latinx (Arellano-Morales et al., 2015; Pérez et al., 2008; Todorova et al., 2010), and approximately 30 percent of Multicultural immigrants of Southeast Asian, or African backgrounds (Tran et al., 2010) reported experiencing discrimination in their lifetime. While aspects of the discrimination Multicultural people face may be similar to that faced by racial minorities who do not identify as Multicultural, discrimination as perpetual foreigners, microaggressions, and the association between discrimination and acculturative stress and acculturation may be specific to Multicultural Americans.

6.2.1 Perpetual Foreigner Stereotype

Many Multicultural people experience discrimination when they are stereotyped as perpetual foreigners despite self-identification as American (Armenta et al., 2013; Huynh et al., 2011; Liang et al., 2004; Tuan, 1998). These experiences are driven by perceptions that Multicultural Americans do not match ideal American values, behaviors, or beliefs (Armenta et al., 2013). Perpetual foreigner stereotypes are communicated through questions about where one is really from, or through comments on one's English proficiency (Armenta et al., 2013; Cheryan & Monin, 2005). Though these experiences can be ambiguous, identity questioning experiences are perceived as more discriminatory by Multicultural people within an anti-immigration context (Albuja et al., 2019b). This suggests people may view these stereotypes as a symptom of a broader unwelcoming social context. Perpetual foreigner stereotypes are also communicated through more direct forms of identity denial, where Multicultural people's identity as American is challenged (Albuja et al., 2019a; Cheryan & Monin, 2005). Such views of Multicultural Americans as perpetual foreigners may lead to perceptions of them as disloyal to the US, particularly in the context of intergroup threat (Kunst et al., 2019).

Stereotyping as foreign, and related discrimination, can also occur based on Multicultural people's language use (Cobas & Feagin, 2008). For example, Chinese American adolescents' stronger self-reported accent was associated with more frequent experiences of discrimination and stereotyping as a foreigner (Kim et al., 2011). Similarly, Latinx Americans who primarily spoke Spanish reported more discrimination than those who were bilingual or primarily spoke English (National Survey of Latinos, 2002). Language discrimination can lead to everyday discrimination, such as a lack of service in restaurants due to limited English proficiency (Zhang et al., 2012). Latinx adolescents also reported being treated poorly due to being monolingual English speakers, including feeling pressured to speak better Spanish (Romero & Roberts, 2003). Finally, discrimination based on language can also be institutional, such as through restricted access to health care for people with limited English proficiency (Ayón & Becerra, 2013; Yoo et al., 2009). Together, this suggests Multicultural people face discrimination because they are seen as foreigners in the US, which may be especially salient based on their language use and proficiency.

6.2.2 Microaggressions

Multicultural people also experience microaggressions, often aimed at their subordinated status or at their perceived cultural foreignness (Nadal et al., 2014; Rivera et al., 2010, 2016). Rivera et al. (2010) created a taxonomy of micro-aggressions against Latinxs, including low intelligence, subordination, pathology of cultural values, mistreatment due to language and accent use, being treated as not American enough, criminality, and invalidation of the Latinx experience. Other work has identified exoticization, environmental, and work-place/school microaggressions as common experiences for Latinx Americans (Bonifacio et al., 2018; Nadal et al., 2014). Microaggressions among Asian Americans include similar themes, such as exoticization (particularly of women for White American men), and pathologizing of cultural values, as well as different themes, such as ascription of high intelligence in support of the model-minority myth, and invalidation of differences within the pan-ethnic Asian American group (Nadal et al., 2015).

6.2.3 Discrimination and Acculturative Stress

Discrimination of Multicultural people has been conceptualized as an aspect of Multicultural, or acculturative stress (Benet-Martínez & Haritatos, 2005; Huynh et al., 2018; Romero et al., 2007). Acculturative stress describes the stressors of navigating two sets of cultural values, norms, and prescriptions (LaFromboise et al., 1993). Within this framework, discrimination is one factor of acculturative stress among others, including work challenges, language skills, intercultural relations, and cultural isolation (Miller et al., 2011). As a factor of acculturative stress, discrimination can include being treated differently or unfairly because of one's ethnic background. However, there is conceptual variability in the literature, with other studies measuring discrimination as a construct separate from acculturative stress (e.g., Araújo Dawson & Panchanadeswaran, 2010). Within this framework, greater acculturative stress (measured as family conflict and stress related to immigration, marriage, parents, and occupation) was associated with more frequent experiences of everyday discrimination, daily racial discrimination, and major racist events (Araújo Dawson & Panchanadeswaran, 2010). Indeed, the association between discrimination and psychological distress was found to be mediated by acculturative stress (Torres et al., 2012). Finally, among Latinx immigrants, both greater acculturative stress and discrimination are associated with poorer physical health through increased anxiety (Cariello et al., 2020).

Beyond acculturative stress, greater acculturation to the US is associated with more frequent discrimination. This is theorized to occur because people who are more acculturated have more interactions with cultural outgroup members and can detect biases better (Araújo Dawson & Suarez, 2018; Arellano-Morales et al., 2015; Cook et al., 2009; Pérez et al., 2008; Todorova et al., 2010). Yet, some work has only found this association among immigrant participants and has found the opposite association (i.e., greater acculturation was associated with less discrimination) among US-born participants (Finch et al., 2000). An additional study found that Multicultural and bilingual Latinx people reported more frequent discrimination than Latinx people who were more acculturated and English-dominant, and Latinx people who were less acculturated and Spanish-dominant (Salas-Wright et al., 2015), suggesting the relationship between acculturation and discrimination may be nonlinear, and may depend on additional factors such as generational status.

6.2.4 Well-Being Correlates of Discrimination

More frequent discrimination has been associated with greater depression, anxiety, and stress among both adults (Araújo Dawson, 2009; Gee et al., 2007, 2009; Jang et al., 2010; Lee & Ahn, 2011; Miller et al., 2011; Tran et al., 2010) and adolescents (Benhke et al., 2011; Piña-Watson et al., 2015). The association between discrimination and poorer mental health was mediated by a lower sense of control (Jang et al., 2010). Discrimination was also related to physical health, an association that was mediated by poorer sleep among first-generation Latinx immigrants (Green et al., 2021) and by psychological distress among Chinese, Pilipino, and Vietnamese Americans (Mereish et al., 2012). These associations are moderated by the density of ingroup members in partici-pants' neighborhoods (Syed & Juan, 2011) and the degree of ethnic identifica-tion for US-born Asian Americans (Yip et al., 2008). Moreover, more frequent discrimination has been linked with greater substance use among African-born Black, Southeast Asian, and Latinx immigrant adults (Salas-Wright et al., 2015; Tran et al., 2010). Finally, awareness of the perpetual foreigner stereotype and more frequent microaggressions were associated with poorer well-being among adults (Huynh et al., 2011; Nadal et al., 2015; Torres & Taknint, 2015) and adolescents (Huynh, 2012; Kim et al., 2011).

6.2.5 Identity Correlates of Discrimination

For Multicultural people, discrimination is associated with different orien-tations toward one's Multicultural identity. More frequent discrimination was associated with a less harmonious and complementary Multicultural identity (Firat & Noels, 2021; Huynh et al., 2018). However, some work found no association between discrimination and identity harmony among first-generation Multicultural people (Huynh et al., 2018). A meta-analysis found a weak negative association between discrimination and cultural identity for Asian American participants, suggesting Asian Americans who experienced greater discrimination identified less with Asian culture (Lee & Ahn, 2011). Consistent with the rejection-identification and rejection-disidentification models, discrimination among Multicultural people was associated with a stronger ethnic identity and weaker identification with mainstream American culture (sometimes referred to as a national identity; Hakim et al., 2018). Similarly, among Latinxs in the US, being rejected by other Latinxs for their Latinx identity was associated with a weaker Latinx identity and a marginally stronger Multicultural identity, demonstrating people may come to identify with a third culture after rejection (Branscombe et al., 1999; Wiley, 2013).

6.3 Comparing Multiracial and Multicultural Discrimination

The association between discrimination and poorer well-being was both consistent across Multiracial and Multicultural populations, and consistent with various theoretical perspectives. For example, symbolic interactionism (Goffman, 1963) posits that stigmatization can be internalized, and reduce people's well-being and sense of belonging (Baumeister & Leary, 1995). Indeed, across both populations, more frequent experiences of discrimination were associated with poorer mental and physical health, and greater substance use. Among Multiracial people, these associations were moderated and mediated by identity integration, and emergent research has begun to consider the moderating role of ecological context such as subjective racial diversity (Gabriel et al., 2021; Jackson et al., 2012; Reid Marks et al., 2020). Among Multicultural people, these associations were mediated by poorer sleep (Green et al., 2021), and moderated by participants' ethnic identity, and the density of ingroup members in the ecological context (Syed & Juan, 2012; Yip et al., 2008). One study directly comparing Multiracial and Multicultural populations found decreased social belonging to be a consistent mediator of the association between identity denial and depressive symptoms and stress (Albuja et al., 2019a). Future research would benefit from clarifying the role of identity integration as a mediator, moderator, or both in the association between discrimination and well-being. Additionally, greater focus on contextual variables such as ingroup density, racial and cultural diversity, and social cohesion would advance an understanding of how the social context can perpetuate or attenuate discrimination for these populations.

Although both populations shared similar experiences and outcomes of discrimination, there may be differences in what drives discrimination toward Multiracial and Multicultural people. For example, people expect Multiracial children to be less well-adjusted than monoracial children because of their complex racial background (Brandell, 1998). People of color reported more positive attitudes toward Multiracial children than White people (Jackman et al., 2001) and more positive attitudes toward Multiracial children were associated with a stronger ethnic identity and better psychological adjustment among Multiracial adults (Adams, 2008). Relatedly, Multiracial adults reported warmer feelings toward Multiracial people than White, Black, Latinx, or Asian adults, and warmer feelings were associated with less conservative beliefs (Campbell & Herman, 2010). Beyond this initial work, there is a dearth of understanding of what drives attitudes toward Multiracial people. Although Multiracial people's identity and phenotypic racial ambiguity often disrupts people's concepts of race by reducing endorsement of ideologies of race as biological and a topic that should be avoided (Gaither et al., 2019; Young et al., 2013), it is unclear how these or other racial ideologies relate to negative attitudes toward Multiracial people. In contrast, negative attitudes toward Multicultural people may stem from perceived symbolic and realistic threats (Stephan & Stephan, 1996; Stephan et al., 1999). Symbolic threats threaten "the American way of life," such as through the perception that Multicultural people are not assimilating to the US, and are associated with higher right-wing authoritarianism (i.e., individual obedience to authorities and adherence to traditional norms and values; Altemeyer, 1988; Duckitt, 2001). Realistic threats threaten people's material resources, such as through the perception that Multicultural people are taking jobs in the US, and are associated with higher social dominance orientation (i.e., individual preference for social hierarchies; Duckitt, 2001; Pratto et al., 1994). Thus, although there is evidence for ideological and trait underpinnings of attitudes toward Multicultural people, less is known about similar drivers of attitudes toward Multiracial people. Future research would benefit from understanding whether attitudes toward Multiracial people are similarly driven by perceived symbolic threats (e.g., perceived threats to the current racial hierarchy) and realistic threats (e.g., perceived threats to resources through an expanded application of affirmative action; Good et al., 2010; Sanchez et al., 2011).

Generational status is often considered in studies of discrimination among Multicultural populations, and some work has found generational status to be an important moderator. For example, the negative association between discrimination and identity harmony was only found among second generation, but not among first generation, Multicultural people (Huynh et al., 2018). Similarly, the association between acculturation and discrimination was positive among second-generation Multicultural Americans, but negative among first-generation Multicultural Americans (Finch et al., 2000). The experiences of first- and second-generation Multicultural people may differ in a variety of ways, including in their Multicultural identity orientation (Huynh et al., 2018), experiences of discrimination (Huynh et al., 2018), and vulnerability to identity denial (Wang et al., 2013). Future research would benefit from additional consideration of generational differences in Multicultural people's experiences of microaggressions, and the association between various types of discrimination and well-being. In contrast, generational status is not often considered in research on Multiracial discrimination. Some definitions of Multiracial do not include later generation Multiracial people, but multigenerational Multiracial people who continue to identify as Multiracial may be especially interested in maintaining their ties to their multiple racial backgrounds and may experience discrimination differently than first-generation Multiracial people (Song, 2021). Future research may consider the role of generational status in the discrimination experiences of Multiracial people.

Some microaggressions were similar between the populations. For example, both Multiracial and Multicultural people experience exoticization and exclusion (Johnston & Nadal, 2010; Rivera et al., 2010). Microaggressions based on lower status were also shared between some Multiracial and Multicultural populations, though Multicultural Asian Americans are often stereotyped as high-status rather than low status (Johnston & Nadal, 2010; Nadal et al., 2015). Multicultural microaggressions also focused more on values than multiracial microaggressions. For example, Multicultural people reported that their cultural values and speaking style were pathologized, while for Multiracial people, pathologizing microaggressions focused on perceptions of them as confused about their identity rather than focused on their values. While both populations may experience similar microaggressions, including pathologizing from others, there may be differences in the content of the microaggressions. Relatedly, Multiracial people reported experiencing identity denial more often and identity questioning less often than Multicultural people, suggesting race may be policed more strictly than culture, but foreigner stereotypes may be especially relevant to questions Multicultural people face. Future research may seek to better understand the impact of these various types of microaggressions across both populations through methods that allow for the study of the cumulative impact of these experiences over time, rather than testing one isolated event.

There was evidence consistent with rejection-identification theory among both Multiracial and Multicultural samples (Giamo et al., 2012; Wiley, 2013). Indeed, people may come to identify more strongly as Multiracial or

Multicultural when either these identities, or their monoracial or monocultural identities are rejected. However, evidence of this among Multicultural people is weaker and should be replicated in future research. Future research should also systematically test the implications of rejection for each identity, including a Multiracial or Multicultural identity, and how these vary based on the background of the perpetrator, as this would clarify how rejection-identification and rejection-disidentification theories apply to these populations.

Qualitative research has identified various ways that Multiracial people may cope with discrimination, including through avoidance, anger, advocacy, seeking community, and shifting racial identities (Snyder, 2016). Yet, antidiscrimination policies in the US currently do not apply specifically to Multiracial populations, and there is opposition among the lay public to include Multiracial in antidiscrimination laws (Campbell & Herman, 2010). Nevertheless, Multiracial people demonstrate resilience and resistance to discrimination through appreciation of human differences and pride in being Multiracial (Salahuddin & O'Brien, 2011). Similarly, Multicultural people have shown resistance and resilience when facing discrimination (Casanova, 2012). For example, through a strong identity, and through support from family and mentors, Multicultural people are able to foster resilience processes in the face of discrimination (Casanova, 2012; Sajquim de Torres & Lusk, 2018). Multicultural people also show resilience and resistance to discrimination through civic engagement, such as participating in protests and community organizing (Suárez-Orozco et al., 2015). Future research could test targeted interventions to help Multiracial and Multicultural people foster greater resilience through Multiracial and Multicultural pride, and through support from others.

7 General Discussion

In sum, increased growth of Multiracial and Multicultural populations in the US has been followed by increased research on the psychological experiences of these groups. The history of Multiracial and Multicultural people in the US includes restriction and subjugation through legislation, as well as social creation and re-creation of racial categories through institutions such as the census (Davis, 1991; Hochschild & Powell, 2008; Snipp, 2003; Sohoni, 2007). In parallel with these historical developments, the study of Multiracial people (especially Multiracial identity development research), and Multicultural people (especially acculturation research) began with more restrictive, negative perspectives that have since developed to become more flexible, ecological and dynamic (Berry, 1997; Campbell & Eggerling-Boeck, 2006; Charmaraman et al., 2014; Hong et al., 2000; Kahn & Denmon, 1997; Rockquemore et al., 2009; Rudmin, 2003; Shih & Sanchez, 2005; West et al., 2017). Across both populations and literatures, the sociopolitical climate shaped the focus of research on these groups, particularly through the research questions and theoretical frameworks used. An important implication of this finding is that the current sociopolitical climate is influencing contemporary experiences of and attitudes toward Multiracial and Multicultural people. For example, a recent rise in anti-immigration policies may influence the amount of discrimination Multicultural people face, catalyze socialization among young people, or create perceptions of cultural conflict. Current research should account for the sociopolitical climate, and study how the current zeitgeist is influencing Multiracial and Multicultural people's identity processes and experiences. Moreover, immigration policies must consider the needs of both host and immigrating populations in order to reduce the stigmatization and discrimination of Multicultural people. Similarly, national rhetoric on immigration that acknowledges the US tradition of immigration and immigrants' positive contributions may help improve the climate for Multicultural people. Relatedly, allowing flexibility in racial identification options would promote autonomy for Multiracial people, and policymakers could directly report how people who selected multiple racial options were treated in data analysis (e.g., whether Multiracial people were considered an individual group, whether subgroups were accounted for, whether Multiracial people were included as members of a monoracial group, or another analytic option). Increasing transparency in this reporting would help policymakers be more informed consumers of information and better understand how Multiracial people are represented in any findings.

Given differences in the historical and theoretical roots of research with Multiracial and Multicultural people, it is unsurprising to find methodological differences as well. Multiracial research has focused on self-identification and others' racial categorization through both correlational and experimental methods, while multicultural research has overwhelmingly focused on acculturation, primarily through correlational and longitudinal methods (Bierwiaczonek & Kunst, 2021; Charmaraman et al., 2014; Rudmin et al., 2017). These methods share similar challenges in defining inclusion criteria and dynamically capturing people's identities (Charmaraman et al., 2014; Nguyen & Benet-Martínez, 2007; Shih & Sanchez, 2005; Song, 2021). As a result, these methods share limitations such as the common exclusion of Multiracial or Multicultural people who do not identify with those labels, and the little experimental causal evidence of mechanisms of how identity is shaped, and how it influences well-being or other outcomes. Yet, by studying these populations, researchers have advanced a more thoughtful approach to identity that accounts for external and internal dynamics. It would be informative to expand this work to decenter Whiteness and move beyond a majority/minority cultural framework through a focus on people who have two minority backgrounds (Garay & Remedios, 2021; Verkuyten, 2018).

We also explored family and peer socialization, which includes dimensions shared across both Multiracial and Multicultural people, such as cultural socialization, preparation for bias, egalitarianism, and promotion of mistrust (Hughes et al., 2006). Socialization diverges in ways that are more specific to each population, such as through Multiracial identity socialization or transmission of cultural values (Ayón, 2016; Harris et al., 2013). As the Multiracial and Multicultural youth populations continue to grow, this work underscores the importance of teaching children about race and culture in ways that are flexible and inclusive, and the importance of research that incorporates the various socialization agents through whom children may learn about their various backgrounds. The work reviewed suggests parents should discuss race and culture explicitly with their children in ways that promote autonomy and flexibility, and emphasize the social constructive nature of these categories. Identities may also be negotiated in similar ways with respect to the level of involvement in each racial or cultural group (Berry, 1997; Roccas & Brewer, 2002). Finally, there is ample evidence that both populations are discriminated against, both interpersonally and structurally (Franco et al., 2021a; Miller et al., 2012) based on the existence of each group's multiple identities and ingroups. This implies that for both populations, the process of identity negotiation may be a challenging and/or fulfilling experience, and one that is impacted by the stigmatization of others. The prevalence of discrimination calls for greater research to understand the impact of this discrimination, and interventions to improve societal attitudes toward these populations. For example, legal protections against discrimination could be updated to include Multiracial and Multicultural populations. Similarly, Multiracial and Multicultural people's eligibility for diversity-promoting programs such as affirmative action should be considered and communicated to the public. Understanding the impact of discrimination is especially relevant to practitioners, who should understand the unique experiences, opportunities, and challenges Multiracial and Multicultural people face in order to better serve these individuals. For example, understanding the cumulative effect of repeated identity denial or questioning experiences can help practitioners teach Multiracial and Multicultural people positive coping skills and prevent maladaptive coping such as alcohol use (Albuja et al., 2022).

Taken together, we have identified and summarized areas of overlap and divergence in each domain of research reviewed (see Table 1). The areas of

Table 1 Summary of comparative findings between multiracial and multicultural literatures

	Similarities	Differences
History	• Initial approaches applied monoracial and monocultural frameworks and focused on a monoracial or monocultural low-status identity as the optimal identity outcome. • The next wave of research focused on dynamic and ecological approaches to understanding Multiracial and Multicultural identity.	• Multiracial research studied identity dynamics through longitudinal and self-reported methods, while multicultural research studied identity dynamics though situational fluidity and frame-switching. • Multiracial research has directly compared Multiracial and monoracial populations, while this approach is less common in research with Multicultural populations. • Current focus for multiracial research is on the structural forces impacting Multiracial people, whereas for Multicultural populations research focuses on dynamic processes of identity negotiation.
Methods	• How to define and operationalize Multiracial and Multicultural identity has been a central challenge, leading to heterogeneity across studies.	• Multicultural research has a stronger tradition of incorporating measurement invariance in studies than multiracial research.

Socialization	• A central aim has been to study identity development processes and correlates of identity and well-being. • Research with both populations is often grounded in bioecological theories of child development. • Similar socializing agents are studied, with grandparents playing an important role.	• Multiracial research has focused on how people are categorized by others, thus centering phenotype as a central variable, while multicultural research mostly focuses on individuals' acculturation and identity integration. • Multiracial research focuses on identity socialization and interracial intergroup relations, while multicultural research focuses on transmission of cultural values. • Multiracial socialization often focuses on socialization to the "Multiracial" label, while research on cultural identity often studies people's identification with their ethnic identity (e.g., Latinx American or Asian American) rather than with a "Multicultural" identity.
Identity Negotiation	• Researchers created typologies to categorize people's relation to each racial or cultural background. • Other typologies also represent how people negotiate each of their backgrounds. • Both fields have most recently moved away from typologies in favor of considering identity negotiation	• Typologies in Multiracial identity focused more on specific racial combinations (e.g., Black/White) whereas Multicultural identity has focused on a more general dichotomy of heritage versus mainstream cultures.

Table 1 (cont.)

Similarities	Differences
strategies as dynamic processes and mechanisms for the effects of multiraciality and multiculturalism.	• Greater consideration of intersectionality and phenotypic presentation in Multiracial identity (i.e., effects of one identity moderated by another) than Multicultural identity. • Greater focus on the commonalities among Multicultural individuals based on the identity negotiation processes they use instead of their specific cultural combinations compared to research with Multiracial people.
Discrimination • Discrimination is similarly associated with well-being across both populations. • Both populations experienced similar microaggressions, and demonstrated similar responses to rejection. • Both populations have demonstrated resilience and resistance to systems of oppression and discrimination.	• Less is known about ideological drivers of discrimination against Multiracial people, while discrimination against Multicultural people is often driven by perceptions of symbolic or realistic threat. • The moderating role of generational status has been studied more among Multicultural people than Multiracial people.

overlap support the argument that some identity experiences, and how they have been studied, are shared across Multiracial and Multicultural populations who hold two identities within one shared identity domain. For example, researchers' focus on uncovering the "optimal" identity for well-being, and the recurring challenges in defining and operationalizing Multiracial and Multicultural identities were seen across both literatures. These experiences may be unique to people who hold two identities simultaneously in one domain, and highlight the nuances in defining racial and cultural experiences for people who blend across groups. This provides a fruitful area for theoretical development to identify the underlying causes for these challenges, the specificity and generality of these experiences, and whether boundary conditions extend beyond race and culture.

Relatedly, the areas of difference indicate both meaningful distinctions between race and culture, as well as needed directions for additional research. It is important to remember these groups are distinct in some ways, even if definitions of identity remain mixed. For example, the focus on transmission of cultural values within the socialization of Multicultural people speaks to qualitative differences between cultural and racial identities. The role of phenotypic presentation and categorization of Multicultural people has received scant research attention, so it is currently unclear whether similar categorization heuristics and predictors are found among both populations. This, and similar open questions, demonstrate a promising area for future research.

8 Conclusions

The research reviewed here demonstrates the heterogeneity within these populations and undermines perceptions of these groups as monoliths. Often, researchers and institutions collect data in a format that allows for multiple identifications, but that same data are analyzed with only monoracial categories (Sanchez et al., 2020). This approach may obscure meaningful differences between groups in how identities are conceptualized and experienced. Yet, this approach is also representative of the many challenges researchers face when studying these populations given that these research questions necessitate that we move beyond previous frameworks and theories to grapple with identity as flexible, malleable, and influenced both by internal factors and external perceptions. The varied definitions and operationalizations are meaningful. For example, whether Multiracial is operationalized to be US-born dictates whether Multiracial might be differentiated from Multicultural (Albuja et al., 2019a). This illustrates the social constructive nature of race and culture, which is always in flux and being redefined.

Researchers stand to gain a deeper understanding of race and culture by studying Multiracial and Multicultural groups both separately and jointly, and should also consider their own role in the definition and redefinition of these constructs. Together, Multiracial and Multicultural people demonstrate how identities are powerfully shaped by others' categorization and perceptions, and how both internal and external factors are iterative in identity processes. This work encourages deeper thinking about identity as multidimensional by encompassing values, practices, behaviors, and presentation into our definitions of identity development. Shared limitations across the literatures are seen in the lack of experimental tests of the effect of exposure to different races and cultures on identity, well-being, and life experiences such as political participation. Future research would benefit from greater use of longitudinal and experimental methods to address the causality of many of these observed relationships (Bierwiaczonek & Kunst, 2021). Moreover, moving forward, researchers seeking to integrate this work must consider internal and external factors in how identity is negotiated. Similarly, researchers must consider inclusion criteria and whether the same sample would qualify at another point in time, or in another setting, and the consequences of these identity experiences for well-being and lived experience.

References

Adams, P. J. (2008). Comparing biracials and monoracials: Psychological well-being and attitudes toward multiracial people (Unpublished doctoral dissertation, The Ohio State University).

Albuja, A. F., Ansari, S., Ortiz-Payne, M. et al. (2022). Demographic and regional differences in caregivers' ethnic-racial socialization of young children [Manuscript submitted for publication].

Albuja, A. F., Gaither, S. E., Sanchez, D. T., Straka, B., & Cipollina, R. (2019). Psychophysiological stress responses to bicultural and biracial identity denial. *Journal of Social Issues*, *75*(4), 1165–1191.

Albuja, A. F., Sanchez, D. T., & Gaither, S. E. (2018). Fluid racial presentation: Perceptions of contextual "passing" among biracial people. *Journal of Experimental Social Psychology*, *77*, 132–142.

Albuja, A. F., Sanchez, D. T., & Gaither, S. E. (2019a). Identity denied: Comparing American or White identity denial and psychological health outcomes among bicultural and biracial people. *Personality and Social Psychology Bulletin*, *45*(3), 416–430. https://doi.org/10.1177/0146167218788553.

Albuja, A. F., Sanchez, D. T., & Gaither, S. E. (2019b). Identity questioning: Antecedents and consequences of prejudice attributions. *Journal of Social Issues*, *75*(2), 515–537.

Albuja, A. F., Sanchez, D. T., & Gaither, S. E. (2020). Intra-race intersectionality: Identity denial among dual-minority biracial people. *Translational Issues in Psychological Science*, *6*(4), 392–403.

Albuja, A. F., Straka, B., Desjardins, M., Swartzwelder, H. S., & Gaither, S. E. (2021). Alcohol use and related consequences for monoracial and multiracial Native American/American Indian college students. *Experimental and Clinical Psychopharmacology*, *29*(5), 487–500.

Aldoney, D., & Cabrera, N. J. (2016). Raising American citizens: Socialization goals of low-income immigrant Latino mothers and fathers of young children. *Journal of Child and Family Studies*, *25*(12), 3607–3618.

Altemeyer, B. (1988). *Enemies of freedom: Understanding right-wing authoritarianism*. Jossey-Bass.

Alwin, D. F. (1991). Family of origin and cohort differences in verbal ability. *American Sociological Review*, *56*(5), 625–638.

Amaro, H., & Zambrana, R. E. (2000). Criollo, Mestizo, Mulato, Latinegro, Indigena, White, or Black? The US Hispanic/Latino population and multiple responses in the 2000 census. *American Journal of Public Health, 90,* 1724–1726.

American Civil Liberties Union. (n.d.). Map: The leadup to Loving. www.aclu .org/other/map-leadup-loving.

American Psychological Association. (2006). Maria P. P. Root, PhD: Clinical psychologist and independent scholar. *Monitor on Psychology, 37*(2), 55.

Amiot, C. E., De la Sablonniere, R., Terry, D. J., & Smith, J. R. (2007). Integration of social identities in the self: Toward a cognitive-developmental model. *Personality and Social Psychology Review, 11*(4), 364–388.

Araújo, B. Y., & Borrell, L. N. (2006). Understanding the link between discrimination, mental health outcomes, and life chances among Latinos. *Hispanic Journal of Behavioral Sciences, 28*(2), 245–266.

Araújo Dawson, B. (2009). Discrimination, stress, and acculturation among Dominican immigrant women. *Hispanic Journal of Behavioral Sciences, 31* (1), 96–111.

Araújo Dawson, B., & Panchanadeswaran, S. (2010). Discrimination and acculturative stress among first-generation Dominicans. *Hispanic Journal of Behavioral Sciences, 32*(2), 216–231.

Araújo Dawson, B., & Suárez, Z. E. (2018). How does transnationalism affect the perceptions of discrimination among Dominicans, Puerto Ricans and Cubans? *Journal of Human Behavior in the Social Environment, 28*(2), 162–176.

Arellano-Morales, L., Roesch, S. C., Gallo, L. C. et al. (2015). Prevalence and correlates of perceived ethnic discrimination in the Hispanic Community Health Study/Study of Latinos Sociocultural Ancillary Study. *Journal of Latina/o Psychology, 3*(3), 160–176.

Arends-Tóth, J., & Van de Vijver, F. J. (2004). Domains and dimensions in acculturation: Implicit theories of Turkish–Dutch. *International Journal of Intercultural Relations, 28*(1), 19–35.

Armenta, B. E., Lee, R. M., Pituc, S. T. et al. (2013). Where are you from? A validation of the foreigner objectification scale and the psychological correlates of foreigner objectification among Asian Americans and Latinos. *Cultural Diversity and Ethnic Minority Psychology, 19*(2), 131–142. https:// doi.org/10.1037/a0031547.

Atkin, A. L., Christophe, N. K., Stein, G. L., Gabriel, A. K., & Lee, R. M. (2022). Race terminology in the field of psychology: Acknowledging the growing multiracial population in the U.S. *American Psychologist, 77*(3), 381–393. https://doi.org/10.1037/amp0000975.

Atkin, A. L., & Jackson, K. F. (2021). "Mom, you don't get it": A critical examination of Multiracial emerging adults' perceptions of parental support. *Emerging Adulthood, 9*(4), 305–319.

Atkin, A. L., & Yoo, H. C. (2019). Familial racial-ethnic socialization of multiracial American youth: A systematic review of the literature with MultiCrit. *Developmental Review, 53*, 100869.

Ayón, C. (2016). Talking to Latino children about race, inequality, and discrimination: Raising families in an anti-immigrant political environment. *Journal of the Society for Social Work and Research, 7*(3), 449–477.

Ayón, C., & Becerra, D. (2013). Mexican immigrant families under siege: The impact of anti-immigrant policies, discrimination, and the economic crisis. *Advances in Social Work, 14*(1), 206–228.

Ayón, C., Nieri, T., & Ruano, E. (2020). Ethnic-racial socialization among Latinx families: A systematic review of the literature. *Social Service Review, 94*(4), 693–747.

Batalova, J., Hanna, M., & Levesque, C. (2021). Frequently requested statistics on immigrants and immigration in the United States. *Migration Policy Institute.* www.migrationpolicy.org/article/frequently-requested-statistics-immigrants-and-immigration-united-states-2020.

Baumeister, R. F., & Leary, M. R. (1995). The need to belong: Desire for interpersonal attachments as a fundamental human motivation. *Psychological Bulletin, 117*(3), 497–529.

Behnke, A. O., Plunkett, S. W., Sands, T., & Bámaca-Colbert, M. Y. (2011). The relationship between Latino adolescents' perceptions of discrimination, neighborhood risk, and parenting on self-esteem and depressive symptoms. *Journal of Cross-Cultural Psychology, 42*(7), 1179–1197.

Benet-Martínez, V., & Haritatos, J. (2005). Bicultural identity integration (BII): Components and psychosocial antecedents. *Journal of Personality, 73*(4), 1015–1050.

Benet-Martínez, V., Leu, J., Lee, F., & Morris, M. W. (2002). Negotiating Multiculturalism: Cultural frame switching in Multiculturals with oppositional versus compatible cultural identities. *Journal of Cross-Cultural Psychology, 33*(5), 492–516.

Benet-Martínez, V., Lee, F., & Leu, J. (2006). Biculturalism and cognitive complexity: Expertise in cultural representations. *Journal of Cross-Cultural Psychology, 37*(4), 386–407.

Bennett, C. (2000). Racial categories used in the decennial censuses, 1790 to the present. *Government Information Quarterly, 17*(2), 161–180.

Berry, J. W. (1974). Psychological aspects of cultural pluralism: Unity and identity reconsidered. *Topics in Culture Learning, 2*, 17–22.

Berry, J. W. (1980). Acculturation as varieties of adaptation. In A. Padilla (Ed.), *Acculturation: Theory, models and findings* (pp. 9–25). Westview.

Berry, J. W. (1997). Immigration, acculturation, and adaptation. *Applied Psychology, 46*(1), 5–34.

Berry, J. W. (2009). A critique of critical acculturation. *International Journal of Intercultural Relations, 33*(5), 361–371.

Berry, J. W., Lepshokova, Z., Collaboration, M., Grigoryev, D. Annis, R. C., Au, A. K., & Ziaian, T. (2022). How shall we all live together? Meta-analytical review of the mutual intercultural relations in plural societies project. *Applied Psychology, 71*(3), 1014–1041.

Berry, J. W., Phinney, J. S., Sam, D. L., & Vedder, P. (2006). Immigrant youth: Acculturation, identity, and adaptation. *Applied Psychology, 55*(3), 303–332.

Berry, J. W., & Sam, D. L. (1997). Acculturation and adaptation. In J. W. Berry, M. H. Segall, & C. Kagitcibasi (Eds.), *Handbook of cross-cultural psychology, Vol. 3. Social behaviour and applications* (2nd ed., pp. 291–326). Allyn & Bacon.

Bierwiaczonek, K., & Kunst, J. R. (2021). Revisiting the integration hypothesis: Correlational and longitudinal meta-analyses demonstrate the limited role of acculturation for cross-cultural adaptation. *Psychological Science, 32*(9), 1476–1493.

Birman, D., & Simon, C. D. (2014). Acculturation research: Challenges, complexities, and possibilities. In F. T. L. Leong, L. Comas-Díaz, G. C. Nagayama Hall, V. C. McLoyd, & J. E. Trimble (Eds.), *APA handbook of multicultural psychology, Vol. 1. Theory and research* (pp. 207–230). American Psychological Association.

Bonifacio, L., Gushue, G. V., & Mejia-Smith, B. X. (2018). Microaggressions and ethnic identity in the career development of Latina college students. *The Counseling Psychologist, 46*(4), 505–529.

Bowles, D. D. (1993). Bi-racial identity: Children born to African-American and White couples. *Clinical Social Work Journal, 21*(4), 417–428.

Boyd, R., & Richerson, P. J. (2005). *The origin and evolution of cultures.* Oxford University Press.

Brackett, K. P., Marcus, A., McKenzie, N. J., Mullins, L. C., Tang, Z., & Allen, A. M. (2006). The effects of multiracial identification on students' perceptions of racism. *The Social Science Journal, 43*(3), 437–444. https://doi.org/10.1016/j.soscij.2006.04.01

Branscombe, N. R., Ellemers, N., Spears, R., & Doosje, B. (1999). The context and content of social identity threat. In N. Ellemers, R. Spears, & B. Doosje (Eds.), *Social identity: Context, commitment, content* (pp. 35–58). Blackwell Science.

Brandell, J. R. (1988). Treatment of the biracial child: Theoretical and clinical issues. *Journal of Multicultural Counseling and Development, 16*(4), 176–187.

Brittian, A. S., Umaña-Taylor, A. J., & Derlan, C. L. (2013). An examination of biracial college youths' family ethnic socialization, ethnic identity, and adjustment: Do self-identification labels and university context matter? *Cultural Diversity and Ethnic Minority Psychology, 19*(2), 177–189.

Bronfenbrenner, U., & Morris, P. A. (2006). The bioecological model of human development. In R. M. Lerner (Ed.), *Handbook of child psychology, Vol. 1. Theoretical models of human development* (6th ed., pp. 793–828). Wiley.

Browning, J. R. (1951). Anti-miscegenation laws in the United States. *Duke Bar Journal, 1*(1), 26–41.

Calderón-Tena, C. O., Knight, G. P., & Carlo, G. (2011). The socialization of prosocial behavioral tendencies among Mexican American adolescents: The role of familism values. *Cultural Diversity and Ethnic Minority Psychology, 17*(1), 98–106.

Campbell, M. E., & Eggerling-Boeck, J. (2006). "What about the children?" The psychological and social well-being of multiracial adolescents. *The Sociological Quarterly, 47*(1), 147–173.

Campbell, M. E., & Herman, M. R. (2010). Politics and policies: Attitudes toward multiracial Americans. *Ethnic and Racial Studies, 33* (9), 1511–1536.

Cano, M. Á., Schwartz, S. J., Castillo, L. G. et al. (2016). Health risk behaviors and depressive symptoms among Hispanic adolescents: Examining acculturation discrepancies and family functioning. *Journal of Family Psychology, 30* (2), 254–265.

Cardwell, M. E., Soliz, J., Crockett, L. J., & Bergquist, G. L. (2020). Critical incidents in the development of (multi) ethnic-racial identity: Experiences of individuals with mixed ethnic-racial backgrounds in the US. *Journal of Social and Personal Relationships, 37*(5), 1653–1672.

Cariello, A. N., Perrin, P. B., Williams, C. D. et al. (2020). Moderating influence of enculturation on the relations between minority stressors and physical health via anxiety in Latinx immigrants. *Cultural Diversity and Ethnic Minority Psychology, 26*(3), 356–366.

Carranza, M. E. (2007). Building resilience and resistance against racism and discrimination among Salvadorian female youth in Canada. *Child & Family Social Work, 12*(4), 390–398.

Carter, G. (2013). *The United States of the united races: A Utopian history of racial mixing.* New York University Press.

Casanova, S. (2012). The stigmatization and resilience of a female indigenous Mexican immigrant. *Hispanic Journal of Behavioral Sciences, 34*(3), 375–403.

Chancler, L. L., Webb, F. J., & Miller, C. (2017). Role of the Black grandmother in the racial socialization of their biracial grandchildren. *Marriage & Family Review*, *53*(5), 444–464.

Chao, M. M., Hong, Y. Y., & Chiu, C. Y. (2013). Essentializing race: Its implications on racial categorization. *Journal of Personality and Social Psychology*, *104*(4), 619–634.

Charmaraman, L., Woo, M., Quach, A., & Erkut, S. (2014). How have researchers studied multiracial populations? A content and methodological review of 20 years of research. *Cultural Diversity and Ethnic Minority Psychology*, *20*(3), 336–352.

Cheah, C. S., Leung, C. Y., & Zhou, N. (2013). Understanding "tiger parenting" through the perceptions of Chinese immigrant mothers: Can Chinese and US parenting coexist? *Asian American Journal of Psychology*, *4*(1), 30–40.

Chen, J. M. (2019). An integrative review of impression formation processes for multiracial individuals. *Social and Personality Psychology Compass*, *13*(1), e12430.

Chen, J. M., Kteily, N. S., & Ho, A. K. (2019). Whose side are you on? Asian Americans' mistrust of Asian–White biracials predicts more exclusion from the ingroup. *Personality and Social Psychology Bulletin*, *45*(6), 827–841.

Cheng, C. Y., Hanek, K. J., Odom, A. C., & Lee, F. (2021). Divided loyalties: Identity integration and cultural cues predict ingroup favoritism among biculturals. *International Journal of Intercultural Relations*, *80*, 321–335.

Cheng, C. Y., Sanchez-Burks, J., & Lee, F. (2008). Connecting the dots within: Creative performance and identity integration. *Psychological Science*, *19*(11), 1178–1184.

Cheng, C.-Y., & Lee, F. (2009). Multiracial identity integration: Perceptions of conflict and distance among multiracial individuals. *Journal of Social Issues*, *65*(1), 51–68.

Cheng, C.-Y., Lee, F., & Benet-Martínez, V. (2006). Assimilation and contrast effects in cultural frame switching: Bicultural identity integration and valence of cultural cues. *Journal of Cross-Cultural Psychology*, *37*(6), 742–760.

Cheryan, S., & Monin, B. (2005). Where are you really from? Asian Americans and identity denial. *Journal of Personality and Social Psychology*, *89*(5), 717–730.

Chiao, J. Y., Heck, H. E., Nakayama, K., & Ambady, N. (2006). Priming race in biracial observers affects visual search for Black and White faces. *Psychological Science*, *17*(5), 387–392.

Chirkov, V. (2009). Critical psychology of acculturation: What do we study and how do we study it, when we investigate acculturation? *International Journal of Intercultural Relations*, *33*(2), 94–105.

Choi, Y., Harachi, T. W., Gillmore, M. R., & Catalano, R. F. (2006). Are multiracial adolescents at greater risk? Comparisons of rates, patterns, and correlates of substance use and violence between monoracial and multiracial adolescents. *American Journal of Orthopsychiatry*, *76*(1), 86–97.

Christophe, N. K., Atkin, A. L., Stein, G. L., & Chan, M. (2021). Examining Multiracial pride, identity-based challenges, and discrimination: An exploratory investigation among Biracial emerging adults. *Race and Social Problems*. Advanced online publication. https://doi.org/10.1007/s12552-021-09325-4

Citlak, B., Leyendecker, B., Schölmerich, A., Driessen, R., & Harwood, R. L. (2008). Socialization goals among first-and second-generation migrant Turkish and German mothers. *International Journal of Behavioral Development*, *32*(1), 56–65.

Cobas, J. A., & Feagin, J. R. (2008). Language oppression and resistance: The case of middle class Latinos in the United States. *Ethnic and Racial Studies*, *31*(2), 390–410.

Cohen, A. B. (2009). Many forms of culture. *American Psychologist*, *64*(3), 194–204.

Collins, J. F. (2000). Biracial Japanese American identity: An evolving process. *Cultural Diversity and Ethnic Minority Psychology*, *6*(2), 115–133.

Contrada, R. J., Ashmore, R. D., Gary, M. L. et al. (2001). Measures of ethnicity-related stress: Psychometric properties, ethnic group differences, and associations with well-being. *Journal of Applied Social Psychology*, *31*(9), 1775–1820.

Cook, B., Alegria, M., Lin, J. Y., & Guo, J. (2009). Pathways and correlates connecting Latinos' mental health with exposure to the United States. *American Journal of Public Health*, *99*(12), 2247–2254.

Cooney, T. M., & Radina, M. E. (2000). Adjustment problems in adolescence: Are multiracial children at risk? *American Journal of Orthopsychiatry*, *70*(4), 433–444.

Cross, F. (2022). Documentation status socialization as an ethnic-racial socialization dimension: Incorporating the experience of mixed-status Latinx families. *Studies in Social Justice*, *16*(1), 264–279.

Cross, F. L., Martinez, S. B., & Rivas-Drake, D. (2021). Documentation status socialization among Latinx immigrant parents. *New Directions for Child and Adolescent Development*, *2021*(177), 31–49.

Cross, W. E. (1987). A two-factor theory of Black identity: Implications for the study of identity development in minority children. In J. Phinney & M. Rotheram (Eds.), *Children's ethnic socialization: Pluralism and development* (pp. 117–133). Sage.

Cross, W. E., Jr., & Cross, T. B. (2008). Theory, research, and models. In S. M. Quintana & C. McKown (Eds.), *Handbook of race, racism, and the developing child* (pp. 154–181). Wiley.

Csizmadia, A. (2011). The role of racial identification, social acceptance/rejection, social cognition, and racial socialization in multiracial youth's positive development. *Sociology Compass, 5*(11), 995–1004.

Daniel, G. R. (1992). Passers and pluralists: Subverting the racial divide. In M. P. P. Root (Ed.), *Racially mixed people in America* (pp. 91–107). Sage.

Davenport, L. D. (2016). The role of gender, class, and religion in biracial Americans' racial labeling decisions. *American Sociological Review, 81*(1), 57–84.

Davis, F. J. (1991). *Who is Black?* Penn State University Press.

Deaux, K., & Ethier, K. A. (1998). Negotiating social identity. In J. K. Swim & C. Stangor (Eds.), *Prejudice: The target's perspective* (pp. 301–323). Academic Press.

De Leersnyder, J. (2017). Emotional acculturation: A first review. *Current Opinion in Psychology, 17*, 67–73.

Deci, E. L., & Ryan, R. M. (2012). Self-determination theory. In P. A. M. Van Lange, A. W. Kruglanski, & E. T. Higgins (Eds.), *Handbook of theories of social psychology* (pp. 416–436). Sage.

DeFina, R., & Hannon, L. (2016). Social status attainment and racial category selection in the contemporary United States. *Research in Social Stratification and Mobility, 44*, 91–97.

Devos, T., & Banaji, M. R. (2005). American = White? *Journal of Personality and Social Psychology, 88*(3), 447–466.

Devos, T., & Ma, D. S. (2008). Is Kate Winslet more American than Lucy Liu? The impact of construal processes on the implicit ascription of a national identity. *British Journal of Social Psychology, 47*(2), 191–215.

Devos, T., Gavin, K., & Quintana, F. J. (2010). Say "adios" to the American dream? The interplay between ethnic and national identity among Latino and Caucasian Americans. *Cultural Diversity and Ethnic Minority Psychology, 16*(1), 37–49.

Dickter, C. L., & Kittel, J. A. (2012). The effect of stereotypical primes on the neural processing of racially ambiguous faces. *Social Neuroscience, 7*(6), 622–631.

Doucerain, M., Dere, J., & Ryder, A. G. (2013). Travels in hyper-diversity: Multiculturalism and the contextual assessment of acculturation. *International Journal of Intercultural Relations*, *37*(6), 686–699.

Downie, M., Koestner, R., ElGeledi, S., & Cree, K. (2004). The impact of cultural internalization and integration on well-being among tricultural individuals. *Personality and Social Psychology Bulletin*, *30*(3), 305–314.

Downie, M., Mageau, G. A., Koestner, R., & Liodden, T. (2006). On the risk of being a cultural chameleon: Variations in collective self-esteem across social interactions. *Cultural Diversity and Ethnic Minority Psychology*, *12*(3), 527–540.

Doyle, J. M., & Kao, G. (2007). Are racial identities of multiracials stable? Changing self-identification among single and multiple race individuals. *Social Psychology Quarterly*, *70*(4), 405–423.

Du Bois, W. E. B. (1903). *The souls of Black folk: Essays and sketches*. Fawcett.

Duckitt, J. (2001). A dual-process cognitive-motivational theory of ideology and prejudice. In M. P. Zanna (Ed.), *Advances in experimental social psychology* (Vol. 33, pp. 41–113). Academic Press.

Dunbar, R. I. (1998). The social brain hypothesis. *Evolutionary Anthropology: Issues, News, and Reviews*, *6*(5), 178–190.

Eberhardt, J. L., Dasgupta, N., & Banaszynski, T. L. (2003). Believing is seeing: The effects of racial labels and implicit beliefs on face perception. *Personality and Social Psychology Bulletin*, *29*, 360–370.

Edwards, L. M., & Pedrotti, J. T. (2008). A content and methodological review of articles concerning multiracial issues in six major counseling journals. *Journal of Counseling Psychology*, *55*(3), 411–418.

Erikson, E. H. (1968). Identity: Youth and crisis. New York: W. W. Norton & Company.

Ferguson, G. M. (2013). The big difference a small island can make: How Jamaican adolescents are advancing acculturation science. *Child Development Perspectives*, *7*(4), 248–254.

Ferguson, G. M., Bornstein, M. H., & Pottinger, A. M. (2012). Tridimensional acculturation and adaptation among Jamaican adolescent–mother dyads in the United States. *Child Development*, *83*(5), 1486–1493.

Ferguson, G. M., Iturbide, M. I., & Gordon, B. P. (2014). Tridimensional (3D) acculturation: Ethnic identity and psychological functioning of tricultural Jamaican immigrants. *International Perspectives in Psychology*, *3*(4), 238–251.

Field, L. D. (1996). Piecing together the puzzle: Self-concept and group identity in biracial Black/White youth. In M. P. P. Root (Ed.), *The Multiracial experience: Racial borders as the new frontier* (pp. 211–216). Sage.

Finch, B. K., Kolody, B., & Vega, W. A. (2000). Perceived discrimination and depression among Mexican-origin adults in California. *Journal of Health and Social Behavior, 41*(3), 295–313.

Firat, M., & Noels, K. A. (2021). Perceived discrimination and psychological distress among immigrants to Canada: The mediating role of bicultural identity orientations. *Group Processes & Intergroup Relations*. Advanced online publication. https://doi.org/10.1177/1368430221990082

Franco, M. (2019). Let the racism tell you who your friends are: The effects of racism on social connections and life-satisfaction for Multiracial people. *International Journal of Intercultural Relations, 69*, 54–65.

Franco, M., & Carter, S. (2019). Discrimination from family and substance use for multiracial individuals. *Addictive Behaviors, 92*, 203–207.

Franco, M., Durkee, M., & McElroy-Heltzel, S. (2021a). Discrimination comes in layers: Dimensions of discrimination and mental health for multiracial people. *Cultural Diversity and Ethnic Minority Psychology, 27*(3), 343–353.

Franco, M. G., & Franco, S. A. (2016). Impact of identity invalidation for Black multiracial people: The importance of race of perpetrator. *Journal of Black Psychology, 42*(6), 530–548.

Franco, M. G., Katz, R., & O'Brien, K. M. (2016). Forbidden identities: A qualitative examination of racial identity invalidation for Black/White Biracial individuals. *International Journal of Intercultural Relations, 50*, 96–109.

Franco, M., & McElroy-Heltzel, S. (2019). Let me choose: Primary caregiver cultural humility, racial identity, and mental health for Multiracial people. *Journal of Counseling Psychology, 66*(3), 269–279.

Franco, M. G., & O'Brien, K. M. (2018). Racial identity invalidation with multiracial individuals: An instrument development study. *Cultural Diversity and Ethnic Minority Psychology, 24*(1), 112–125.

Franco, M., Toomey, T., DeBlaere, C., & Rice, K. (2021b). Identity incongruent discrimination, racial identity, and mental health for multiracial individuals. *Counselling Psychology Quarterly, 34*(1), 87–108.

Freeman, J. B., Pauker, K., & Sanchez, D. T. (2016). A perceptual pathway to bias: Interracial exposure reduces abrupt shifts in real-time race perception that predict mixed-race bias. *Psychological Science, 27*(4), 502–517.

Freeman, J. B., Penner, A. M., Saperstein, A., Scheutz, M., & Ambady, N. (2011). Looking the part: Social status cues shape race perception. *PloS One, 6*, e25107.

Friedman, R., Liu, W., Chi, S. C. S., Hong, Y. Y., & Sung, L. K. (2012). Cross-cultural management and bicultural identity integration: When does experience abroad lead to appropriate cultural switching? *International Journal of Intercultural Relations, 36*(1), 130–139.

Gabriel, A. K., Yoo, H. C., Jackson, K. F., & Guevarra, R. P., Jr. (2021). Perceived monoracism and psychological adjustment of multiracial adults: The roles of racially diverse contexts and creating third space. *American Journal of Community Psychology.* Advanced online publication. https://doi.org/10.1002/ajcp.12564

Gaither, S. E., Cohen-Goldberg, A. M., Gidney, C. L., & Maddox, K. B. (2015). Sounding Black or White: Priming identity and biracial speech. *Frontiers in Psychology, 6*(457), 1–11.

Gaither, S. E., Pauker, K., Slepian, M. L., & Sommers, S. R. (2016). Social belonging motivates categorization of racially ambiguous faces. *Social Cognition, 34,* 97–118.

Gaither, S. E., Remedios, J. D., Schultz, J. R., & Sommers, S. R. (2015). Priming White identity elicits stereotype boost for biracial Black-White individuals. *Group Processes & Intergroup Relations, 18*(6), 778–787.

Gaither, S. E., Sommers, S. R., & Ambady, N. (2013). When the half affects the whole: Priming identity for biracial individuals in social interactions. *Journal of Experimental Social Psychology, 49*(3), 368–371.

Gaither, S. E., Toosi, N. R., Babbitt, L. G., & Sommers, S. (2019). Exposure to Biracial faces reduces colorblindness. *Personality and Social Psychology Bulletin, 45*(1), 54–66.

Garay, M. M., & Remedios, J. D. (2021). A review of White-centering practices in multiracial research in social psychology. *Social and Personality Psychology Compass, 15*(10), e12642.

García-Ramírez, M., de la Mata, M. L., Paloma, V., & Hernández-Plaza, S. (2011). A liberation psychology approach to acculturative integration of migrant populations. *American Journal of Community Psychology, 47*(1), 86–97.

Garth, T. R. (1930). A review of race psychology. *Psychological Bulletin, 27*(5), 329–356.

Gartner, M., Kiang, L., & Supple, A. (2014). Prospective links between ethnic socialization, ethnic and American identity, and well-being among Asian-American adolescents. *Journal of Youth and Adolescence, 43*(10), 1715–1727.

Gee, G. C., Ro, A., Shariff-Marco, S., & Chae, D. (2009). Racial discrimination and health among Asian Americans: Evidence, assessment, and directions for future research. *Epidemiologic Reviews, 31*(1), 130–151.

Gee, G. C., Spencer, M., Chen, J., Yip, T., & Takeuchi, D. T. (2007). The association between self-reported racial discrimination and 12-month

DSM–IV mental disorders among Asian Americans nationwide. *Social Science & Medicine, 64*(10), 1984–1996.

Geertz, C. (1973). *The interpretation of cultures* (Vol. 5019). Basic Books.

Giamo, L. S., Schmitt, M. T., & Outten, H. R. (2012). Perceived discrimination, group identification, and life satisfaction among multiracial people: A test of the rejection-identification model. *Cultural Diversity and Ethnic Minority Psychology, 18*(4), 319–328.

Gibbs, J. T., & Moskowitz-Sweet, G. (1991). Clinical and cultural issues in the treatment of biracial and Multicultural adolescents. *Families in Society, 72* (10), 579–592.

Gigli, K. H. (2021). Data disaggregation: A research tool to identify health inequities. *Journal of Pediatric Health Care, 35*(3), 332–336.

Goffman, E. (1963). Embarrassment and social organization. In N. J. Smelser & W. T. Smelser (Eds.), *Personality and social systems* (pp. 541–548). John Wiley.

Gonzalez-Barrera, A., & Lopez, M. H. (2015). Is being Hispanic a matter of race, ethnicity or both? *Pew Research Center.* www.pewresearch.org/fact-tank/2015/06/15/is-being-hispanic-a-matter-of-race-ethnicity-or-both/.

Good, J. J., Chavez, G. F., & Sanchez, D. T. (2010). Sources of self-categorization as minority for mixed-race individuals: Implications for affirmative action entitlement. *Cultural Diversity and Ethnic Minority Psychology, 16* (4), 453–460.

Good, J. J., Sanchez, D. T., & Chavez, G. F. (2013). White ancestry in perceptions of Black/White biracial individuals: Implications for affirmative-action contexts. *Journal of Applied Social Psychology, 43*(S2), E276–E286.

Gordon, M. M. (1964). *Assimilation in American life.* Oxford University Press.

Green, T., Shipman, J., Valrie, C. et al. (2021). Discrimination and health among first-generation Hispanic/Latinx immigrants: The roles of sleep and fatigue. *Journal of Racial and Ethnic Health Disparities,* 1–12.

Grieco, E. M. (2014). The "Second Great Wave" of immigration: Growth of the foreign-born population since 1970. *Random Samplings.* www.census.gov/news room/blogs/random-samplings/2014/02/the-second-great-wave-of-immigration-growth-of-the-foreign-born-population-since-1970.html.

Grigoryev, D., & Berry, J. W. (2022). "Causality crisis" in acculturation research a false alarm? A commentary on Kunst (2021). *International Journal of Intercultural Relations, 86,* 158–162.

Grove, K. J. (1991). Identity development in interracial, Asian/White late adolescents: Must it be so problematic? *Journal of Youth and Adolescence, 20*(6), 617–628.

Guo, X., Suarez-Morales, L., Schwartz, S. J., & Szapocznik, J. (2009). Some evidence for multidimensional biculturalism: Confirmatory factor analysis and measurement invariance analysis on the Bicultural involvement questionnaire–short version. *Psychological Assessment, 21*(1), 22–31.

Hakim, N. H., Molina, L. E., & Branscombe, N. R. (2018). How discrimination shapes social identification processes and well-being among Arab Americans. *Social Psychological and Personality Science, 9*(3), 328–337.

Hamako, E. (2014). Improving anti-racist education for multiracial students (unpublished doctoral dissertation, University of Massachusetts Amherst). http://scholarworks.umass.edu/dissertations_2/90/.

Harris, D. R., & Sim, J. J. (2002). Who is multiracial? Assessing the complexity of lived race. *American Sociological Review, 67*(4), 614–627.

Harris, J. C. (2016). Toward a critical multiracial theory in education. *International Journal of Qualitative Studies in Education, 29*(6), 795–813.

Harris, J. C. (2017a). Multiracial college students' experiences with multiracial microaggressions. *Race Ethnicity and Education, 20*(4), 429–445.

Harris, J. C. (2017b). Multiracial microaggressions: Narratives of Multiracial student affairs professionals. *Journal of College Student Development, 58*(7), 1055–73.

Harris, J. C., Snider, J. C., Anderson, J. L., & Griffin, K. A. (2021). Multiracial faculty members' experiences with multiracial microaggressions. *American Journal of Education, 127*(4), 531–561.

Harris, K., Henriksen, R. C., Jr., & Onwuegbuzie, A. J. (2013). Counseling single mothers of multiple heritage children: What is the difference? *The Family Journal, 21*(4), 396–401.

Haslam, S. A., Turner, J. C., Oakes, P. J., & McGarty, C. (1992). Context-dependent variation in social stereotyping 1: The effects of intergroup relations as mediated by social change and frame of reference. *European Journal of Social Psychology, 22*, 3–20.

Heine, S. J. (2015). *Cultural psychology: Third international student edition.* WW Norton.

Heine, S. J., Lehman, D. R., Markus, H. R., & Kitayama, S. (1999). Is there a universal need for positive self-regard? *Psychological Review, 106*(4), 766–794.

Herman, M. (2004). Forced to choose: Some determinants of racial identification in multiracial adolescents. *Child Development, 75*(3), 730–748.

Herman, M. R. (2020). Methods of measuring Multiracial Americans. In Z. L. Rocha & P. J. Aspinall (Eds.), *The Palgrave international handbook of mixed racial and ethnic classification* (pp. 95–111). Palgrave Macmillan.

Herring, R. D. (1995). Developing biracial ethnic identity: A review of the increasing dilemma. *Journal of Multicultural Counseling and Development, 23*(1), 29–38.

Higgins, E. T. (1996). Knowledge activation: Accessibility, applicability, and salience. In E. T. Higgins & A. W. Kruglanski (Eds.), *Social psychology: Handbook of basic principles* (pp. 133–168). Guilford.

Hitlin, S., Brown, J. S., & Elder, G. H., Jr. (2007). Measuring Latinos: Racial vs. ethnic classification and self-understandings. *Social Forces, 86*(2), 587–611.

Hitlin, S., Scott Brown, J., & Elder, G. H., Jr. (2006). Racial self-categorization in adolescence: Multiracial development and social pathways. *Child Development, 77*(5), 1298–1308.

Ho, A. K., Kteily, N. S., & Chen, J. M. (2020). Introducing the sociopolitical motive × intergroup threat model to understand how monoracial perceivers' sociopolitical motives influence their categorization of multiracial people. *Personality and Social Psychology Review, 24*(3), 260–286.

Ho, A. K., Roberts, S. O., & Gelman, S. A. (2015). Essentialism and racial bias jointly contribute to the categorization of multiracial individuals. *Psychological Science, 26*(10), 1639–1645.

Ho, A. K., Sidanius, J., Cuddy, A. J., & Banaji, M. R. (2013). Status boundary enforcement and the categorization of Black–White biracials. *Journal of Experimental Social Psychology, 49*(5), 940–943.

Hochschild, J. L., & Powell, B. M. (2008). Racial reorganization and the United States census 1850–1930: Mulattoes, half-breeds, mixed parentage, Hindoos, and the Mexican race. *Studies in American Political Development, 22*(1), 59–96.

Hong, Y., & Schmidt, C. (2021). Multiculturalism and cultural assimilation. *Oxford Research Encyclopedia of Psychology*.

Hong, Y.-y. (2013). A dynamic constructivist approach to culture: Moving from describing culture to explaining culture. In R. Wyer, C.-y. Chiu, & Y.-y. Hong (Eds.), *Understanding culture* (pp. 18–38). Psychology Press.

Hong, Y.- y., Morris, M. W., Chiu, C.- y., & Benet-Martínez, V. (2000). Multicultural minds: A dynamic constructivist approach to culture and cognition. *American Psychologist, 55*(7), 709–720.

Hugenberg, K., & Bodenhausen, G. V. (2004). Ambiguity in social categorization: The role of prejudice and facial affect in race categorization. *Psychological Science, 15*(5), 342–345.

Hughes, D., Rodriguez, J., Smith, E. P. et al. (2006). Parents' ethnic-racial socialization practices: A review of research and directions for future study. *Developmental Psychology, 42*(5), 747–770.

Huguley, J. P., Wang, M.-T., Vasquez, A. C., & Guo, J. (2019). Parental ethnic–racial socialization practices and the construction of children of color's ethnic–racial identity: A research synthesis and meta-analysis. *Psychological Bulletin, 145*(5), 437–458.

Hurtado, S., Alvarado, A. R., & Guillermo-Wann, C. (2015). Thinking about race: The salience of racial identity at two-and four-year colleges and the climate for diversity. *The Journal of Higher Education, 86*(1), 127–155.

Huynh, Q. L., Benet-Martínez, V., & Nguyen, A. M. D. (2018). Measuring variations in bicultural identity across US ethnic and generational groups: Development and validation of the bicultural identity integration scale – version 2 (BIIS-2). *Psychological Assessment, 30*(12), 1581–1596.

Huynh, Q. L., Devos, T., & Smalarz, L. (2011). Perpetual foreigner in one's own land: Potential implications for identity and psychological adjustment. *Journal of Social and Clinical Psychology, 30*(2), 133–162.

Huynh, Q. L., Nguyen, A. M. D., & Benet-Martínez, V. (2011). Bicultural identity integration. In S. J. Schwartz, K. Luyckx, & V. L. Vignoles (Eds.), *Handbook of identity theory and research* (pp. 827–842). Springer.

Huynh, V. W. (2012). Ethnic microaggressions and the depressive and somatic symptoms of Latino and Asian American adolescents. *Journal of Youth and Adolescence, 41*(7), 831–846.

Ifekwunigwe, J. O. (2004). Introduction: Rethinking "mixed race" studies. In J. O. Ifekwunigwe (Ed.), *"Mixed race" studies: A reader* (pp. 1–29). Routledge.

Jackman, C. F., Wagner, W. G., & Johnson, J. T. (2001). The attitudes toward multiracial children scale. *Journal of Black Psychology, 27*(1), 86–99.

Jackson, K. F. (2009). Beyond race: Examining the facets of multiracial identity through a life- span developmental lens. *Journal of Ethnic and Cultural Diversity in Social Work, 18*(4), 309–326.

Jackson, K. F., Mitchell, F. M., Snyder, C. R., & Samuels, G. E. M. (2020). Salience of ethnic minority grandparents in the ethnic-racial socialization and identity development of multiracial grandchildren. *Identity, 20*(2), 73–91.

Jackson, K. F., Wolven, T., & Crudup, C. (2019). Parental ethnic-racial socialization in multiracial Mexican families. *Journal of Ethnic & Cultural Diversity in Social Work, 28*(2), 165–190.

Jackson, K. F., Yoo, H. C. B., Guevarra, R., Jr., & Harrington, B. A. (2012). Role of identity integration on the relationship between perceived racial discrimination and psychological adjustment of multiracial people. *Journal of Counseling Psychology, 59*(2), 240–250.

Jacobs, J. H. (1992). Identity development in biracial children. In M. P. P. Root (Ed.), *Racially mixed people in America* (pp. 190–206). Sage.

Jang, Y., Chiriboga, D. A., Kim, G., & Rhew, S. (2010). Perceived discrimination, sense of control, and depressive symptoms among Korean American older adults. *Asian American Journal of Psychology, 1*(2), 129–135.

John, A., & Montgomery, D. (2012). Socialization goals of first-generation immigrant Indian parents: A Q-methodological study. *Asian American Journal of Psychology, 3*(4), 299–312.

Johnson, R. C., & Nagoshi, C. T. (1986). The adjustment of offspring of within-group and interracial/intercultural marriages: A comparison of personality factor scores. *Journal of Marriage and the Family, 48*(2), 279–284.

Johnston, M. P., & Nadal, K. L. (2010). Multiracial microaggressions: Exposing monoracism in everyday life and clinical practice. In D. W. Sue (Ed.), *Microaggressions and marginality: Manifestation, dynamics, and impact* (pp. 123–144). John Wiley.

Jones, N., Marks, R., Ramirez, R., & Ríos-Vargas, M. (2020). 2020 census illuminates racial and ethnic composition of the country. *US Census America Counts: Stories Behind the Numbers.* www.census.gov/library/stories/2021/08/improved-race-ethnicity-measures-reveal-united-states-population-much-more-multiracial.html.

Kahn, J. S., & Denmon, J. (1997). An examination of social science literature pertaining to multiracial identity. *Journal of Multicultural Social Work, 6*(1–2), 117–138.

Kerwin, C., Ponterotto, J. G., Jackson, B. L., & Harris, A. (1993). Racial identity in biracial children: A qualitative investigation. *Journal of Counseling Psychology, 40*(2), 221–231.

Khanna, N. (2010). "If you're half black, you're just black": Reflected appraisals and the persistence of the one-drop rule. *The Sociological Quarterly, 51* (1), 96–121.

Kich, G. K. (1992). The developmental process of asserting a biracial, Multicultural identity. In M. P. P. Root (Ed.), *Racially mixed people in America* (pp. 304–317). Sage.

Kim, S. Y., Chen, S., Hou, Y., Zeiders, K. H., & Calzada, E. J. (2019). Parental socialization profiles in Mexican-origin families: Considering cultural socialization and general parenting practices. *Cultural Diversity and Ethnic Minority Psychology, 25*(3), 439–450.

Kim, S. Y., & Hou, Y. (2016). Intergenerational transmission of tridimensional cultural orientations in Chinese American families: The role of Multicultural socialization. *Journal of Youth and Adolescence, 45*(7), 1452–1465.

Kim, S. Y., Wang, Y., Deng, S., Alvarez, R., & Li, J. (2011). Accent, perpetual foreigner stereotype, and perceived discrimination as indirect links between English proficiency and depressive symptoms in Chinese American adolescents. *Developmental Psychology, 47*(1), 289–301.

King, A. R. (2013). Mixed messages: How primary agents of socialization influence adolescent females who identify as multiracial–bisexual. *Journal of LGBT Youth, 10*(4), 308–327.

Knight, G. P., Berkel, C., Umaña-Taylor, A. J. et al. (2011). The familial socialization of culturally related values in Mexican American families. *Journal of Marriage and Family, 73*(5), 913–925.

Knight, G. P., Bernal, M. E., Cota, M. K., Garza, C. A., & Ocampo, K. A. (1993a). Family socialization and Mexican American identity and behavior. In M. E. Bernal & G. P. Knight (Eds.), *Ethnic identity: Formation and transmission among Hispanics and other minorities* (pp. 105–129). State University of New York Press.

Knight, G. P., Bernal, M. E., Garza, C. A., Cota, M. K., & Ocampo, K. A. (1993b). Family socialization and the ethnic identity of Mexican-American children. *Journal of Cross-Cultural Psychology, 24*(1), 99–114.

Knight, G. P., Carlo, G., Mahrer, N. E., & Davis, A. N. (2016). The socialization of culturally related values and prosocial tendencies among Mexican-American adolescents. *Child Development, 87*(6), 1758–1771.

Koneru, V. K., Weisman de Mamani, A. G., Flynn, P. M., & Betancourt, H. (2007). Acculturation and mental health: Current findings and recommendations for future research. *Applied and Preventative Psychology, 12*(2), 76–96.

Kosic, A., & Phalet, K. (2006). Ethnic categorization of immigrants: The role of prejudice, perceived acculturation strategies and group size. *International Journal of Intercultural Relations, 30*(6), 769–782.

Krosch, A. R., Berntsen, L., Amodio, D. M., Jost, J. T., & Van Bavel, J. J. (2013). On the ideology of hypodescent: Political conservatism predicts categorization of racially ambiguous faces as Black. *Journal of Experimental Social Psychology, 49*, 1196–1203.

Krosch, A. R., Park, S. J., Walker, J., & Lisner, A. R. (2022). The threat of a majority-minority US alters white Americans' perception of race. *Journal of Experimental Social Psychology, 99*, 104266.

Krosch, A., & Amodio, D. M. (2014). Economic scarcity alters the perception of race. *Proceedings of the National Academies of Science, 111*(25), 9079–9084.

Kteily, N., Cotterill, S., Sidanius, J., Sheehy-Skeffington, J., & Bergh, R. (2014). "Not one of us": Predictors and consequences of denying in-group characteristics to ambiguous suspects. *Personality and Social Psychology Bulletin, 40*(10), 1231–1247.

Kulish, A. L., Cavanaugh, A., Stein, G. L. et al. (2019). Ethnic-racial socialization in Latino families: The influence of mothers' socialization practices on adolescent private regard, familism, and perceived ethnic-racial discrimination. *Cultural Diversity and Ethnic Minority Psychology, 25*(2), 199–209.

Kunst, J. R. (2021). Are we facing a "causality crisis" in acculturation research? The need for a methodological (r)evolution. *International Journal of Intercultural Relations, 85*, A4–A8.

Kunst, J. R., Dovidio, J. F., & Dotsch, R. (2018). White look-alikes: Mainstream culture adoption makes immigrants "look" phenotypically White. *Personality and Social Psychology Bulletin, 44*(2), 265–282.

Kunst, J. R., Lefringhausen, K., Sam, D. L., Berry, J. W., & Dovidio, J. F. (2021). The missing side of acculturation: How majority-group members relate to immigrant and minority-group cultures. *Current Directions in Psychological Science, 30*(6), 485–494.

Kunst, J. R., Thomsen, L., & Dovidio, J. F. (2019). Divided loyalties: Perceptions of disloyalty underpin bias toward dually-identified minority-group members. *Journal of Personality and Social Psychology, 117*(4), 807–838.

LaFromboise, T., Coleman, H. L., & Gerton, J. (1993). Psychological impact of biculturalism: Evidence and theory. *Psychological Bulletin, 114*(3), 395–412.

Lee, D. L., & Ahn, S. (2011). Racial discrimination and Asian mental health: A meta-analysis. *The Counseling Psychologist, 39*(3), 463–489.

Liang, C. T. H., Li, L. C., & Kim, B. S. K. (2004). The Asian American racism-related stress inventory: Development, factor analysis, reliability, and validity. *Journal of Counseling Psychology, 51*(1), 103–114.

Lieber, E., Nihira, K., & Mink, I. T. (2004). Filial piety, modernization, and the challenges of raising children for Chinese immigrants: Quantitative and qualitative evidence. *Ethos, 32*, 324–347.

Liebler, C. A., Porter, S. R., Fernandez, L. E., Noon, J. M., & Ennis, S. R. (2017). America's churning races: Race and ethnicity response changes between census 2000 and the 2010 census. *Demography, 54*(1), 259–284.

Liu, W. M., Liu, R. Z., Garrison, Y. L. et al. (2019). Racial trauma, microaggressions, and becoming racially innocuous: The role of acculturation and White supremacist ideology. *American Psychologist, 74*(1), 143–155.

Lombardo, P. A. (1988). Miscegenation, eugenics, and racism: Historical footnotes to Loving v. Virginia. *UC Davis Law Review, 21*(2), 421–452.

Lou, E., & Lalonde, R. N. (2015). Signs of transcendence? A changing landscape of multiraciality in the 21st century. *International Journal of Intercultural Relations, 45*, 85–95.

Lou, E., Lalonde, R. N., & Wilson, C. (2011). Examining a multidimensional framework of racial identity across different biracial groups. *Asian American Journal of Psychology, 2*(2), 79–90.

Luo, R., Tamis-LeMonda, C. S., & Song, L. (2013). Chinese parents' goals and practices in early childhood. *Early Childhood Research Quarterly, 28*(4), 843–857.

Lusk, E. M., Taylor, M. J., Nanney, J. T., & Austin, C. C. (2010). Biracial identity and its relation to self-esteem and depression in mixed Black/White biracial individuals. *Journal of Ethnic & Cultural Diversity in Social Work, 19*(2), 109–126.

MacLin, O., & Malpass, R. (2001). Racial categorization of faces: The ambiguous race face effect. *Psychology, Public Policy, and Law, 7*, 98–118.

Makarova, E., & Birman, D. (2015). Cultural transition and academic achievement of students from ethnic minority backgrounds: A content analysis of empirical research on acculturation. *Educational Research, 57* (3), 305–330.

Makarova, E., & Birman, D. (2016). Minority students' psychological adjustment in the school context: An integrative review of qualitative research on acculturation. *Intercultural Education, 27*(1), 1–21.

Matsunaga, M., Hecht, M. L., Elek, E., & Ndiaye, K. (2010). Ethnic identity development and acculturation: A longitudinal analysis of Mexican-heritage youth in the Southwest United States. *Journal of Cross-Cultural Psychology, 41*(3), 410–427.

McFarland, A. M., & Fingerhut, A. W. (2011). Cognitive frame switching in biracial Asian/Caucasian individuals. *Journal of Interpersonal Relations, Intergroup Relations and Identity, 4*(1), 63–73.

Mchitarjan, I., & Reisenzein, R. (2015). The culture-transmission motive in immigrants: A world-wide internet survey. *PLoS One, 10*(11), e0141625.

McRoy, R. G., & Freeman, E. (1986). Racial identity issues among mixed-race children. *Children & Schools, 8*(3), 164–174.

Meca, A., Eichas, K., & Schwartz, S. J. (2019). Biculturalism and bicultural identity: A relational model of bicultural systems. In P. F. Titzmann & P. Jugert (Eds.), *Youth in multicultural societies: New directions for future research and interventions* (pp. 41–57). Routledge.

Mereish, E. H., Liu, M. M., & Helms, J. E. (2012). Effects of discrimination on Chinese, Pilipino, and Vietnamese Americans' mental and physical health. *Asian American Journal of Psychology, 3*(2), 91–103.

Merz, E. M., Özeke-Kocabas, E., Oort, F. J., & Schuengel, C. (2009). Intergenerational family solidarity: Value differences between immigrant groups and generations. *Journal of Family Psychology, 23*(3), 291–300.

Meyers, C., Aumer, K., Schoniwitz, A. et al. (2020). Experiences with micro-aggressions and discrimination in racially diverse and homogeneously white contexts. *Cultural Diversity and Ethnic Minority Psychology, 26*(2), 250–259.

Miller, M. J., Kim, J., & Benet-Martínez, V. (2011). Validating the riverside acculturation stress inventory with Asian Americans. *Psychological Assessment, 23*(2), 300–310.

Miller, M. J., Kim, J., Chen, G. A., & Alvarez, A. N. (2012). Exploratory and confirmatory factor analyses of the Asian American racism-related stress inventory. *Assessment, 19*(1), 53–64.

Miville, M. L. (2005). Psychological functioning and identity development of biracial people: A review of current theory and research. In R. T. Carter (Ed.), *Handbook of racial-cultural psychology and counseling* (pp. 295–319). Wiley.

Mok, A., & Morris, M. W. (2009). Cultural chameleons and iconoclasts: Assimilation and reactance to cultural cues in biculturals' expressed personalities as a function of identity conflict. *Journal of Experimental Social Psychology, 45*(4), 884–889.

Mok, A., & Morris, M. W. (2013). Bicultural self-defense in consumer contexts: Self-protection motives are the basis for contrast versus assimilation to cultural cues. *Journal of Consumer Psychology, 23*(2), 175–188.

Museus, S. D., Sariñana, S. A. L., Yee, A. L., & Robinson, T. E. (2016). A qualitative analysis of multiracial students' experiences with prejudice and discrimination in college. *Journal of College Student Development, 57* (6), 680–697.

Nadal, K. L., Mazzula, S. L., Rivera, D. P., & Fujii-Doe, W. (2014). Microaggressions and Latina/o Americans: An analysis of nativity, gender, and ethnicity. *Journal of Latina/o Psychology, 2*(2), 67–78.

Nadal, K. L., Sriken, J., Davidoff, K. C., Wong, Y., & McLean, K. (2013). Microaggressions within families: Experiences of multiracial people. *Family Relations, 62*(1), 190–201.

Nadal, K. L., Wong, Y., Griffin, K. et al. (2011). Microaggressions and the multiracial experience. *International Journal of Humanities and Social Sciences, 1*(7), 36–44.

Nadal, K. L., Wong, Y., Sriken, J., Griffin, K., & Fujii-Doe, W. (2015). Racial microaggressions and Asian Americans: An exploratory study on within-group differences and mental health. *Asian American Journal of Psychology, 6*(2), 136–144.

Nalven, T., Spillane, N. S., & Rossi, J. S. (2021). Racial discrimination, racial identity affiliation, and heavy alcohol use among multiracial individuals. *Alcoholism: Clinical and Experimental Research, 45*(8), 1653–1663.

National Survey of Latinos. (2002). *National survey of Latinos: Summary of findings*. Pew Hispanic Center and Henry J. Kaiser Family Foundation.

Ng, S. H., Han, S., Mao, L., & Lai, J. C. (2010). Dynamic bicultural brains: fMRI study of their flexible neural representation of self and significant others in response to culture primes. *Asian Journal of Social Psychology, 13*(2), 83–91.

Nguyen, A. M. D., & Benet-Martínez, V. (2007). Biculturalism unpacked: Components, measurement, individual differences, and outcomes. *Social and Personality Psychology Compass, 1*(1), 101–114.

Nguyen, A. M. D., & Benet-Martínez, V. (2013). Biculturalism and adjustment: A meta-analysis. *Journal of Cross-Cultural Psychology, 44*(1), 122–159.

No, S., Hong, Y.- y., Liao, H.-Y. et al. (2008). Lay theory of race affects and moderates Asian Americans' responses toward American culture. *Journal of Personality and Social Psychology, 95*(4), 991–1004.

Nobles, M. (2000). *Shades of citizenship: Race and the census in modern politics*. Stanford University Press.

Norman, J. B., & Chen, J. M. (2020). I am Multiracial: Predictors of Multiracial identification strength among mixed ancestry individuals. *Self and Identity, 19*(5), 501–520.

Norman, J. B., Franco, M. G., & Chen, J. M. (2021). Multiracial individuals' experiences of rejection and acceptance from different racial groups and implications for life satisfaction. *The Journal of Social Psychology*. Advanced online publication. https://doi.org/10.1080/00224545.2021.1996322

O'Donoghue, M. (2005). White mothers negotiating race and ethnicity in the mothering of biracial, Black-White adolescents. *Journal of Ethnic and Cultural Diversity in Social Work, 14*(3–4), 125–156.

Orbe, M. P., Harrison, R., III, Kauffman, L. D., & Laurent, V. (2015). Evolutions of cultural contractual understanding: Exploring biracial women's communicative experiences. *Howard Journal of Communications, 26*(4), 422–443.

Ou, Y.- s., & McAdoo, H. P. (1993). Socialization of Chinese American children. In H. P. McAdoo (Ed.), *Family ethnicity: Strength in diversity* (pp. 245–270). Sage.

Oyserman, D., Sakamoto, I., & Lauffer, A. (1998). Cultural accommodation: Hybridity and the framing of social obligation. *Journal of Personality and Social Psychology, 74*(6), 1606–1618.

Ozer, S., & Schwartz, S. J. (2016). Measuring globalization-based acculturation in Ladakh: Investigating possible advantages of a tridimensional acculturation scale. *International Journal of Intercultural Relations, 53*, 1–15.

Paquette, D. (2004). Theorizing the father–child relationship: Mechanisms and developmental outcomes. *Human Development, 47*, 193–219.

Park, R. E. (1928). Human migration and the marginal man. *American Journal of Sociology, 33*(6), 881–893.

Park, R. E. (1931). Mentality of racial hybrids. *American Journal of Sociology, 36*(4), 534–551.

Parker, K., & Barroso, A. (2021). In Vice President Kamala Harris, we can see how America has changed. *Pew Research Center*. www.pewresearch.org/fact-tank/2021/02/25/in-vice-president-kamala-harris-we-can-see-how-america-has-changed/.

Pauker, K., Ambady, N., & Freeman, J. B. (2013). The power of identity to motivate face memory in biracial individuals. *Social Cognition, 31*(6), 780–791.

Pauker, K., Carpinella, C. M., Lick, D. J., Sanchez, D. T., & Johnson, K. L. (2018). Malleability in biracial categorizations: The impact of geographic context and targets' racial heritage. *Social Cognition, 36*(5), 461–480.

Pauker, K., Meyers, C., Sanchez, D. T., Gaither, S. E., & Young, D. M. (2018). A review of multiracial malleability: Identity, categorization, and shifting racial attitudes. *Social and Personality Psychology Compass, 12* (6), e12392.

Pekerti, A. A., Moeller, M., Thomas, D. C., & Napier, N. K. (2015). n-Culturals, the next cross-cultural challenge: Introducing a multicultural mentoring model program. *International Journal of Cross Cultural Management, 15* (1), 5–25.

Pérez, D. J., Fortuna, L., & Alegria, M. (2008). Prevalence and correlates of everyday discrimination among US Latinos. *Journal of Community Psychology, 36*(4), 421–433.

Perreira, K. M., & Pedroza, J. M. (2019). Policies of exclusion: Implications for the health of immigrants and their children. *Annual Review of Public Health, 40*(1), 147–166.

Pew Research Center. (2015a). Modern immigration wave brings 59 million to U.S., driving population growth and change through 2065. www.pewresearch.org/hispanic/2015/09/28/modern-immigration-wave-brings-59-million-to-u-s-driving-population-growth-and-change-through-2065/.

Pew Research Center. (2015b). Multiracial in America: Proud, diverse, and growing in numbers. www.pewresearch.org/social-trends/2015/06/11/multiracial-in-america/.

Piña-Watson, B., Dornhecker, M., & Salinas, S. R. (2015). The impact of bicultural stress on Mexican American adolescents' depressive symptoms and suicidal ideation: Gender matters. *Hispanic Journal of Behavioral Sciences, 37*(3), 342–364.

Pinetta, B. J., Blanco Martinez, S., Cross, F. L., & Rivas-Drake, D. (2020). Inherently political? Associations of parent ethnic–racial socialization and sociopolitical discussions with Latinx youths' emergent civic engagement. *American Journal of Community Psychology, 66*(1–2), 94–105.

Porter, J. R., & Washington, R. E. (1993). Minority identity and self-esteem. *Annual Review of Sociology, 19*(1), 139–161.

Poston, W. C. (1990). The biracial identity development model: A needed addition. *Journal of Counseling & Development, 69*(2), 152–155.

Pratto, F., Sidanius, J., Stallworth, L. M., & Malle, B. F. (1994). Social dominance orientation: A personality variable predicting social and political attitudes. *Journal of Personality and Social Psychology, 67*(4), 741–763.

Priest, N., Walton, J., White, F. et al. (2014). Understanding the complexities of ethnic-racial socialization processes for both minority and majority groups: A 30-year systematic review. *International Journal of Intercultural Relations, 43*(B), 139–155.

Quintana, S. M., & Vera, E. M. (1999). Mexican American children's ethnic identity, understanding of ethnic prejudice, and parental ethnic socialization. *Hispanic Journal of Behavioral Sciences, 21*(4), 387–404.

Ramírez-Esparza, N., Gosling, S. D., Benet-Martínez, V., Potter, J. P., & Pennebaker, J. W. (2006). Do bilinguals have two personalities? A special case of cultural frame switching. *Journal of Research in Personality, 40*(2), 99–120.

Rauktis, M. E., Fusco, R. A., Goodkind, S., & Bradley-King, C. (2016). Motherhood in liminal spaces: White mothers' parenting Black/White children. *Affilia: Journal of Women and Social Work, 31*(4), 434–449.

Redfield, R., Linton, R., & Herskovits, M. J. (1936). Memorandum for the study of acculturation. *American Anthropologist, 38*(1), 149–152.

Reece, R. L. (2019). Coloring racial fluidity: How skin tone shapes multiracial adolescents' racial identity changes. *Race and Social Problems, 11*(4), 290–298.

Reid Marks, L., Thurston, I. B., Kamody, R. C., & Schaeffer-Smith, M. (2020). The role of multiracial identity integration in the relation between racial discrimination and depression in multiracial young adults. *Professional Psychology: Research and Practice, 51*(4), 317–324.

Remedios, J. D., Chasteen, A. L., & Oey, E. (2012). "Unskilled" workers: Social skills stereotypes affect evaluations of biracial job applicants. *Basic and Applied Social Psychology, 34*(3), 204–211.

Richeson, J. A., & Sommers, S. R. (2016). Toward a social psychology of race and race relations for the twenty-first century. *Annual Review of Psychology, 67*, 439–463.

Rivera, D. P., Campón, R. R., & Herbert, K. (2016). The impact of microaggressions and structural inequalities on the well-being of Latina/o American communities. In E. L. Short & L. Wilton (Eds.), *Talking about structural inequalities in everyday life: New politics of race in groups, organizations, and social systems* (pp. 65–83). Information Age.

Rivera, D. P., Forquer, E. E., & Rangel, R. (2010). Microaggressions and the life experience of Latina/o Americans. In D. W. Sue (Ed.), *Microaggressions and marginality: Manifestation, dynamics, and impact* (pp. 59–83). John Wiley.

Roberts, S. O., & Rizzo, M. T. (2020). The psychology of American racism. *American Psychologist, 76*(3), 475–487.

Roccas, S., & Brewer, M. B. (2002). Social identity complexity. *Personality and Social Psychology Review, 6*(2), 88–106.

Rockquemore, K. A. (1999). *Race and identity: Exploring the biracial experience*. University of Notre Dame.

Rockquemore, K. A., & Arend, P. (2002). Opting for White: Choice, fluidity and racial identity construction in post civil-rights America. *Race and Society, 5* (1), 49–64.

Rockquemore, K. A., & Brunsma, D. L. (2002). *Beyond Black: Biracial identity in America*. Sage.

Rockquemore, K. A., & Brunsma, D. L. (2004). Negotiating racial identity: Biracial women and interactional validation. *Women & Therapy, 27*(1–2), 85–102. https://doi.org/10.1300/J015v27n01_06.

Rockquemore, K. A., & Brunsma, D. L. (2007). *Beyond Black: Biracial identity in America*. Rowman & Littlefield.

Rockquemore, K. A., Brunsma, D. L., & Delgado, D. J. (2009). Racing to theory or retheorizing race? Understanding the struggle to build a multiracial identity theory. *Journal of Social Issues, 65*(1), 13–34.

Rockquemore, K., & Laszloffy, T. A. (2005). *Raising biracial children*. Rowman Altamira.

Rodeheffer, C. D., Hill, S. E., & Lord, C. G. (2012). Does this recession make me look Black? The effect of resource scarcity on the categorization of biracial faces. *Psychological Science, 23*(12), 1476–1478.

Romero, A. J., Carvajal, S. C., Valle, F., & Orduña, M. (2007). Adolescent bicultural stress and its impact on mental well-being among Latinos, Asian Americans, and European Americans. *Journal of Community Psychology, 35* (4), 519–534.

Romero, A. J., & Roberts, R. E. (2003). Stress within a bicultural context for adolescents of Mexican descent. *Cultural Diversity and Ethnic Minority Psychology, 9*(2), 171–184.

Root, M. P. (Ed.). (1992). *Racially mixed people in America.* Sage.

Root, M. P. (Ed.). (1996). *The multiracial experience: Racial borders as the new frontier.* Sage.

Root, M. P. P. (2001). Factors influencing the variation in racial and ethnic identity of mixed-heritage persons of Asian ancestry. In T. K. Williams-Leon & C. L. Nakashima (Eds.), *The sum of our parts: Mixed heritage Asian Americans* (pp. 61–70). Temple University.

Root, M. P. P. (2002). Methodological issues in multiracial research. In G. C. Nagayama Hall & S. Okazaki (Eds.), *Asian American psychology: The science of lives in context* (pp. 171–193). American Psychological Association.

Root, M. P. P. (2003). Multiracial families and children: Implications for educational research and practice. *Handbook of Research on Multicultural Education, 2*, 110–124.

Roth, W. D. (2016). The multiple dimensions of race. *Ethnic and Racial Studies, 39*(8), 1310–1338.

Rudmin, F. (2009). Constructs, measurements and models of acculturation and acculturative stress. *International Journal of Intercultural Relations, 33*(2), 106–123.

Rudmin, F. W. (2003). Critical history of the acculturation psychology of assimilation, separation, integration, and marginalization. *Review of General Psychology, 7*(1), 3–37.

Rudmin, F., Wang, B., & de Castro, J. (2017). Acculturation research critiques and alternative research designs. In S. J. Schwartz & J. B. Unger (Eds.), *The Oxford handbook of acculturation and health* (pp. 75–95). Oxford University Press.

Ryder, A. G., Alden, L. E., & Paulhus, D. L. (2000). Is acculturation unidimensional or bidimensional? A head-to-head comparison in the prediction of personality, self-identity, and adjustment. *Journal of Personality and Social Psychology, 79*(1), 49–65.

Saad, C. S., Damian, R. I., Benet-Martínez, V., Moons, W. G., & Robins, R. W. (2013). Multiculturalism and creativity: Effects of cultural context, bicultural identity, and ideational fluency. *Social Psychological and Personality Science, 4*(3), 369–375.

Saad, L. (2017, June 21). Gallup vault: Americans slow to back interracial marriage. *Gallup.* https://news.gallup.com/vault/212717/gallup-vault-americans-slow-back-interracial-marriage.aspx.

Safa, M. D., & Umaña-Taylor, A. J. (2021). Biculturalism and adjustment among US Latinos: A review of four decades of empirical findings. *Advances in Child Development and Behavior, 61,* 73–127.

Sajquim de Torres, M., & Lusk, M. (2018). Factors promoting resilience among Mexican immigrant women in the United States: Applying a positive deviance approach. *Estudios Fronterizos, 19,* 1–20.

Salahuddin, N. M., & O'Brien, K. M. (2011). Challenges and resilience in the lives of urban, multiracial adults: An instrument development study. *Journal of Counseling Psychology, 58*(4), 494–507.

Salas-Wright, C. P., Clark, T. T., Vaughn, M. G., & Córdova, D. (2015). Profiles of acculturation among Hispanics in the United States: Links with discrimination and substance use. *Social Psychiatry and Psychiatric Epidemiology, 50* (1), 39–49.

Sam, D. L., & Ward, C. (2021). Three generations of psychological acculturation research: Theoretical advancements and methodological challenges. In M. Bender & B. G. Adams (Eds.), *Methods and assessment in culture and psychology* (pp. 17–40). Cambridge University Press.

Samelson, F. (1978). From "race psychology" to "studies in prejudice": Some observations on the thematic reversal in social psychology. *Journal of the History of the Behavioral Sciences, 14*(3), 265–278.

Sanchez, D. T., & Bonam, C. M. (2009). To disclose or not to disclose biracial identity: The effect of biracial disclosure on perceiver evaluations and target responses. *Journal of Social Issues, 65*(1), 129–149.

Sanchez, D. T., & Garcia, J. A. (2009). When race matters: Racially stigmatized others and perceiving race as a biological construction affect biracial people's daily well-being. *Personality and Social Psychology Bulletin, 35*(9), 1154–1164.Sanchez, D. T. (2010). How do forced-choice dilemmas affect multiracial people? The role of identity autonomy and public regard in depressive symptoms. *Journal of Applied Social Psychology, 40*(7), 1657–1677.

Sanchez, D. T., Gaither, S. E., Albuja, A. F., & Eddy, Z. (2020). How policies can address multiracial stigma. *Policy Insights from the Behavioral and Brain Sciences, 7*(2), 115–122.

Sanchez, D. T., Good, J. J., & Chavez, G. (2011). Blood quantum and perceptions of Black-White biracial targets: The Black ancestry prototype model of affirmative action. *Personality and Social Psychology Bulletin, 37*(1), 3–14.

Sanchez, D. T., Shih, M., & Garcia, J. A. (2009). Juggling multiple racial identities: Malleable racial identification and psychological well-being. *Cultural Diversity and Ethnic Minority Psychology, 15*(3), 243–254.

Saperstein, A., & Penner, A. M. (2012). Racial fluidity and inequality in the United States. *American Journal of Sociology, 118*(3), 676–727.

Schwartz, S. J., Benet-Martínez, V., Knight, G. P. et al. (2014). Effects of language of assessment on the measurement of acculturation: Measurement equivalence and cultural frame switching. *Psychological Assessment, 26*(1), 100–114.

Schwartz, S. J., Unger, J. B., Baezconde-Garbanati, L. et al. (2015). Longitudinal trajectories of Multicultural identity integration in recently immigrated Hispanic adolescents: Links with mental health and family functioning. *International Journal of Psychology, 50*(6), 440–450.

Schwartz, S. J., Unger, J. B., Zamboanga, B. L., & Szapocznik, J. (2010). Rethinking the concept of acculturation: Implications for theory and research. *American Psychologist, 65*(4), 237–251.

Schwartz, S. J., Vignoles, V. L., Brown, R., & Zagefka, H. (2014). The identity dynamics of acculturation and multiculturalism: Situating acculturation in context. In V. Benet-Martínez & Y.-Y. Hong (Eds.), *The Oxford handbook of multicultural identity* (pp. 57–93). Oxford University Press.

Shih, M., Bonam, C., Sanchez, D., & Peck, C. (2007). The social construction of race: Biracial identity and vulnerability to stereotypes. *Cultural Diversity and Ethnic Minority Psychology, 13*(2), 125–133.

Shih, M., & Sanchez, D. T. (2005). Perspectives and research on the positive and negative implications of having multiple racial identities. *Psychological Bulletin, 131*(4), 569–591.

Shweder, R. A., & Sullivan, M. A. (1993). Cultural psychology: Who needs it? *Annual Review of Psychology, 44*, 497–523.

Sims, J. P. (2012). Beautiful stereotypes: The relationship between physical attractiveness and mixed race identity. *Identities, 19*(1), 61–80.

Skerry, P. (2002). Multiracialism and the administrative state. In J. Perlmann & M. C. Waters (Eds.), *The new race question: How the census counts multiracial individuals* (pp. 327–339). Russell Sage Foundation.

Skinner, A. L., Perry, S. P., & Gaither, S. (2020). Not quite monoracial: Biracial stereotypes explored. *Personality and Social Psychology Bulletin, 46*(3), 377–392.

Snipp, C. M. (2003). Racial measurement in the American census: Past practices and implications for the future. *Annual Review of Sociology, 29*(1), 563–588.

Snyder, C. R. (2012). Racial socialization in cross-racial families. *Journal of Black Psychology, 38*(2), 228–253.

Snyder, C. R. (2016). Navigating in murky waters: How multiracial Black individuals cope with racism. *American Journal of Orthopsychiatry, 86*(3), 265–276.

Sohoni, D. (2007). Unsuitable suitors: Anti-miscegenation laws, naturalization laws, and the construction of Asian identities. *Law & Society Review, 41*(3), 587–618.

Solórzano, D., & Yosso, T. (2001). From racial stereotyping and deficit discourse toward a critical race theory in teacher education. In C. A. Grant & T. K. Chapman (Eds.), *History of multicultural education: Foundations and Stratifications* (pp. 117–129). Routledge.

Song, M. (2021). Who counts as multiracial? *Ethnic and Racial Studies, 44*(8), 1296–1323.

Song, M., & Gutierrez, C. O. N. (2015). "Keeping the story alive": Is ethnic and racial dilution inevitable for multiracial people and their children? *The Sociological Review, 63*(3), 680–698.

Stephan, W. G., & Stephan, C. W. (1996). Predicting prejudice. *International Journal of Intercultural Relations, 20*(3–4), 409–426.

Stephan, W. G., Ybarra, O., & Bachman, G. (1999). Prejudice toward immigrants. *Journal of Applied Social Psychology, 29*(11), 2221–2237.

Stogianni, M., Bender, M., Sleegers, W. W. A., Benet-Martinez, V., & Nguyen, A. (2021). Sample characteristics and country level indicators influencing the relationship between biculturalism and adjustment: An updated meta-analysis. Unpublished Manuscript.

Stokes, M. N., Charity-Parker, B. M., & Hope, E. C. (2021). What does it mean to be Black and White? A meta-ethnographic review of racial socialization in Multiracial families. *Journal of Family Theory & Review, 13*(2), 181–201.

Stone, D., & Dolbin-MacNab, M. (2017). Racial socialization practices of White mothers raising Black-White Biracial children. *Contemporary Family Therapy: An International Journal, 39*(2), 97–111.

Stonequist, E. V. (1937). *The marginal man: A study in personality and culture conflict*. Russell & Russell.

Su, T. F., & Costigan, C. L. (2009). The development of children's ethnic identity in immigrant Chinese families in Canada: The role of parenting practices and children's perceptions of parental family obligation expectations. *The Journal of Early Adolescence, 29*(5), 638–663.

Suárez-Orozco, C., Hernández, M. G., & Casanova, S. (2015). "It's sort of my calling": The civic engagement and social responsibility of Latino immigrant-origin young adults. *Research in Human Development, 12*(1–2), 84–99.

Sue, D. W. (2010). *Microaggressions in everyday life: Race, gender, and sexual orientation*. John Wiley & Sons.

Sui, J., Zhu, Y., & Chiu, C. Y. (2007). Bicultural mind, self-construal, and self-and mother-reference effects: Consequences of cultural priming on recognition memory. *Journal of Experimental Social Psychology, 43*(5), 818–824.

Suinn, R. M., Rickard-Figueroa, K., Lew, S., & Vigil, P. (1987). The Suinn-Lew Asian self-identity acculturation scale: An initial report. *Educational and Psychological Measurement, 47*(2), 401–407.

Syed, M., & Juan, M. J. D. (2012). Discrimination and psychological distress: Examining the moderating role of social context in a nationally representative sample of Asian American adults. *Asian American Journal of Psychology, 3*(2), 104–120.

Szabó, Á., Ward, C., Meca, A., & Schwartz, S. J. (2020). Testing the construct validity and empirical distinctiveness of the multicultural identity styles scale (MISS) and the bicultural identity integration scale (BIIS-2). *Psychological Assessment, 32*(7), 705–712.

Tadmor, C. T., Galinsky, A. D., & Maddux, W. W. (2012a). Getting the most out of living abroad: Biculturalism and integrative complexity as key drivers of creative and professional success. *Journal of Personality and Social Psychology, 103*(3), 520–542.

Tadmor, C. T., Hong, Y.- y., Chao, M. M., Wiruchnipawan, F., & Wang, W. (2012b). Multicultural experiences reduce intergroup bias through epistemic unfreezing. *Journal of Personality and Social Psychology, 103*(5), 750–772.

Tadmor, C. T., & Tetlock, P. E. (2006). Biculturalism: A model of the effects of second-culture exposure on acculturation and integrative complexity. *Journal of Cross-Cultural Psychology, 37*(2), 173–190.

Tadmor, C. T., Tetlock, P. E., & Peng, K. (2009). Acculturation strategies and integrative complexity: The cognitive implications of biculturalism. *Journal of Cross-Cultural Psychology, 40*(1), 105–139.

Tajfel, H., & Turner, J. C. (1979). An integrative theory of intergroup conflict. In M. J. Hatch & M. Schultz (Eds.), *Organizational identity: A reader* (pp. 56–65). Oxford University Press.

Tartakovsky, E. (2009). Cultural identities of adolescent immigrants: A three-year longitudinal study including the pre-migration period. *Journal of Youth and Adolescence, 38*(5), 654–671.

Thompson, D. (2012). Making (mixed-)race: Census politics and the emergence of multiracial multiculturalism in the United States, Great Britain and Canada. *Ethnic and Racial Studies, 35*(8), 1409–1426.

Thornton, M. C. (1996). Hidden agendas, identity theories, and Multiracial people. In M. P. P. Root (Ed.), *The Multiracial experience: Racial borders as the new frontier* (pp. 101–120). Sage.

Titzmann, P. F., & Lee, R. M. (2018). Adaptation of young immigrants: A developmental perspective on acculturation research. *European Psychologist, 23*(1), 72–82.

Todorova, I. L., Falcon, L. M., Lincoln, A. K., & Price, L. L. (2010). Perceived discrimination, psychological distress and health. *Sociology of Health & Illness, 32*(6), 843–861.

Tomishima, S. A. (1999). Factors and experiences in biracial and biethnic identity development (Unpublished doctoral dissertation, The University of Utah).

Torres, L., Driscoll, M. W., & Voell, M. (2012). Discrimination, acculturation, acculturative stress, and Latino psychological distress: A moderated mediational model. *Cultural Diversity and Ethnic Minority Psychology, 18*(1), 17–25.

Torres, L., & Taknint, J. T. (2015). Ethnic microaggressions, traumatic stress symptoms, and Latino depression: A moderated mediational model. *Journal of Counseling Psychology, 62*(3), 393–401.

Townsend, S. S., Markus, H. R., & Bergsieker, H. B. (2009). My choice, your categories: The denial of multiracial identities. *Journal of Social Issues, 65* (1), 185–204.

Tran, A. G., Lee, R. M., & Burgess, D. J. (2010). Perceived discrimination and substance use in Hispanic/ Latino, African-born Black, and Southeast Asian immigrants. *Cultural Diversity and Ethnic Minority Psychology, 16*(2), 226–236.

Tran, A. G. T. T., Miyake, E. R., Martinez-Morales, V., & Csizmadia, A. (2016). "What are you?" Multiracial individuals' responses to racial identification inquiries. *Cultural Diversity and Ethnic Minority Psychology, 22*(1), 26–37. https://doi.org/10.1037/cdp0000031

Tuan, M. (1998). *Forever foreigners or honorary Whites? The Asian ethnic experience today.* Rutgers University Press.

Udry, J. R., Li, R. M., & Hendrickson-Smith, J. (2003). Health and behavior risks of adolescents with mixed-race identity. *American Journal of Public Health, 93*(11), 1865–1870.

Umaña-Taylor, A. J., Alfaro, E. C., Bámaca, M. Y., & Guimond, A. B. (2009). The central role of family socialization in Latino adolescents' cultural orientation. *Journal of Marriage and Family, 71*, 46–60. https://doi.org/10.1111/j.1741-3737.2008.00579.x.

Umaña-Taylor, A. J., Bhanot, R., & Shin, N. (2006). Ethnic identity formation during adolescence: The critical role of families. *Journal of Family Issues, 27* (3), 390–414. https://doi.org/10.1177/0192513X05282960.

Umaña-Taylor, A. J., & Fine, M. A. (2004). Examining ethnic identity among Mexican-origin adolescents living in the United States. *Hispanic Journal of Behavioral Sciences, 26*(1), 36–59.

Umaña-Taylor, A. J., & Hill, N. E. (2020). Ethnic–racial socialization in the family: A decade's advance on precursors and outcomes. *Journal of Marriage and Family*, *82*(1), 244–271.

Umaña-Taylor, A. J., Quintana, S. M., Lee, R. M. et al. (2014). Ethnic and racial identity during adolescence and into young adulthood: An integrated conceptualization. *Child Development*, *85*(1), 21–39.

Umaña-Taylor, A. J., & Yazedjian, A. (2006). Generational differences and similarities among Puerto Rican and Mexican mothers' experiences with familial ethnic socialization. *Journal of Social and Personal Relationships*, *23*(3), 445–464.

Umaña-Taylor, A. J., Zeiders, K. H., & Updegraff, K. A. (2013). Family ethnic socialization and ethnic identity: A family-driven, youth-driven, or reciprocal process? *Journal of Family Psychology*, *27*(1), 137–146.

Uttal, L., & Han, C. y. (2011). Taiwanese immigrant mothers' childcare preferences: Socialization for Multicultural competency. *Cultural Diversity and Ethnic Minority Psychology*, *17*(4), 437–443.

Van Oudenhoven, J. P., & Benet-Martínez, V. (2015). In search of a cultural home: From acculturation to frame-switching and intercultural competencies. *International Journal of Intercultural Relations*, *46*, 47–54.

Vargas, N., & Stainback, K. (2016). Documenting contested racial identities among self-identified Latina/os, Asians, Blacks, and Whites. *American Behavioral Scientist*, *60*(4), 442–464.

Verkuyten, M. (2018). The benefits of studying immigration for social psychology. *European Journal of Social Psychology*, *48*(3), 225–239.

Verkuyten, M., & Pouliasi, K. (2006). Biculturalism and group identification: The mediating role of identification in cultural frame switching. *Journal of Cross-Cultural Psychology*, *37*(3), 312–326.

Vertovec, S. (2007). Super-diversity and its implications. *Ethnic and Racial Studies*, *30*(6), 1024–1054.

Villalobos Solís, M. (2021). Puerto Rican adolescents' visits to the island, familial ethnic socialization, and cultural orientation. *Journal of Social Issues*, *77*(4), 1213–1233.

Wallenstein, P. (2004). *Tell the court I love my wife: Race, marriage, and law: An American history*. Palgrave Macmillan.

Wallman, K. K., Evinger, S., & Schechter, S. (2000). Measuring our nation's diversity: Developing a common language for data on race/ethnicity. *American Journal of Public Health*, *90*(11), 1704–1708.

Wang, J., Minervino, C., & Cheryan, S. (2013). Generational differences in vulnerability to identity denial: The role of group identification. *Group Processes & Intergroup Relations*, *16*(5), 600–617.

Wang, M. T., Smith, L. V., Miller-Cotto, D., & Huguley, J. P. (2020). Parental ethnic-racial socialization and children of color's academic success: A meta-analytic review. *Child Development, 91*(3), e528–e544.

Wang, M.-T., Henry, D. A., Smith, L. V., Huguley, J. P., & Guo, J. (2020). Parental ethnic-racial socialization practices and children of color's psychosocial and behavioral adjustment: A systematic review and meta-analysis. *American Psychologist, 75*(1), 1–22.

Wang, Y., Benner, A. D., & Kim, S. Y. (2015). The cultural socialization scale: Assessing family and peer socialization toward heritage and mainstream cultures. *Psychological Assessment, 27*(4), 1452–1462.

Ward, C., Ng Tseung-Wong, C., Szabo, A., Qumseya, T., & Bhowon, U. (2018). Hybrid and alternating identity styles as strategies for managing multicultural identities. *Journal of Cross-Cultural Psychology, 49*(9), 1402–1439.

Ward, C., Szabó, Á., Schwartz, S. J., & Meca, A. (2021). Acculturative stress and cultural identity styles as predictors of psychosocial functioning in Hispanic Americans. *International Journal of Intercultural Relations, 80*, 274–284.

Wardle, F. (1987). Are you sensitive to interracial children's special identity needs? *Young Children, 42*(2), 53–59.

West, A. L., Muise, A., & Sasaki, J. Y. (2021). The cost of being "true to yourself" for mixed selves: Frame switching leads to perceived inauthenticity and downstream social consequences for Biculturals. *Social Psychological and Personality Science, 12*(5), 829–838.

West, A. L., Zhang, R., Yampolsky, M., & Sasaki, J. Y. (2017). More than the sum of its parts: A transformative theory of biculturalism. *Journal of Cross-Cultural Psychology, 48*(7), 963–990.

Wijeyesinghe, C. L. (2001). Racial identity in multiracial people: An alternative paradigm. In C. L. Wijeyesinghe & B. W. Jackson III (Eds.), *New perspectives on racial identity development: A theoretical and practical anthology* (pp. 129–152). New York University Press.

Wiley, S. (2013). Rejection–identification among Latino immigrants in the United States. *International Journal of Intercultural Relations, 37*(3), 375–384.

Williams, C. B. (1999). Claiming a biracial identity: Resisting social constructions of race and culture. *Journal of Counseling and Development: JCD, 77* (1), 32–35.

Williams, K. (2006). *Mark one or more: Civil rights in Multiracial America*. University of Michigan Press.

Williams-Leon, T., & Nakashima, C. L. (Eds.). (2001). *The sum of our parts: Mixed-heritage Asian Americans*. Temple University Press.

Wilton, L. S., Sanchez, D. T., & Garcia, J. A. (2013). The stigma of privilege: Racial identity and stigma consciousness among biracial individuals. *Race and Social Problems, 5*(1), 41–56.

Woo, M., Austin, S. B., Williams, D. R., & Bennett, G. G. (2011). Reconceptualizing the measurement of multiracial status for health research in the United States. *Du Bois Review: Social Science Research on Race, 8*(1), 25–36.

Wu, C. S., Lee, S. Y., Zhou, X. et al. (2020). Hidden among the hidden: Transracially adopted Korean American adults raising multiracial children. *Developmental Psychology, 56*(8), 1431–1445.

Yampolsky, M. A., Amiot, C. E., & de la Sablonnière, R. (2013). Multicultural identity integration and well-being: A qualitative exploration of variations in narrative coherence and multicultural identification. *Frontiers in Psychology, 4*(126), 1–15.

Yampolsky, M. A., Amiot, C. E., & de la Sablonnière, R. (2016). The multicultural identity integration scale (MULTIIS): Developing a comprehensive measure for configuring one's multiple cultural identities within the self. *Cultural Diversity and Ethnic Minority Psychology, 22*(2), 166–184. https://doi.org/10.1037/cdp0000043

Yampolsky, M. A., West, A. L., Zhou, B., Muise, A., & Lalonde, R. N. (2021). Divided together: How marginalization of intercultural relationships is associated with identity integration and relationship quality. *Social Psychological and Personality Science, 12*(6), 887–897.

Yep, G. A. (2002). My Three Cultures: Navigating the multicultural identity landscape. In J. N. Martin, L. A., Flores, & K. N., Thomas (Eds.), *Readings in cultural contexts* (pp. 79–84). Mountain View: Mayfield.

Yip, T., Gee, G. C., & Takeuchi, D. T. (2008). Racial discrimination and psychological distress: The impact of ethnic identity and age among immigrant and United States-born Asian adults. *Developmental Psychology, 44*(3), 787–800.

Yoo, H. C., Gee, G. C., & Takeuchi, D. (2009). Discrimination and health among Asian American immigrants: Disentangling racial from language discrimination. *Social Science & Medicine, 68*(4), 726–732.

Yoo, H. C., Jackson, K. F., Guevarra, R. P., Jr., Miller, M. J., & Harrington, B. (2016). Construction and initial validation of the multiracial experiences measure (MEM). *Journal of Counseling Psychology, 63*(2), 198–209.

Yoon, E., Chang, C.-T., Kim, S. et al. (2013). A meta-analysis of acculturation/enculturation and mental health. *Journal of Counseling Psychology, 60*(1), 15–30.

Young, D. M., Sanchez, D. T., Pauker, K., & Gaither, S. E. (2021). A meta-analytic review of hypodescent patterns in categorizing multiracial and racially ambiguous targets. *Personality and Social Psychology Bulletin, 47*(5), 705–727.

Young, D. M., Sanchez, D. T., & Wilton, L. S. (2013). At the crossroads of race: Racial ambiguity and biracial identification influence psychological essentialist thinking. *Cultural Diversity and Ethnic Minority Psychology, 19*(4), 461–467.

Zack, N. (Ed.). (1994). *Race and mixed race*. Temple University Press.

Zeiders, K. H., Updegraff, K. A., Umaña-Taylor, A. J., McHale, S. M., & Padilla, J. (2015). Familism values, family time, and Mexican-origin young adults' depressive symptoms. *Journal of Marriage and Family, 78*(1), 91–106.

Zhang, R., Schimel, J., & Faucher, E. H. (2014). Bicultural terror management: Identity hybridity moderates the effect of mortality salience on biculturals' familiarity versus novelty seeking tendency. *Self and Identity, 13*(6), 714–739.

Zhang, W., Hong, S., Takeuchi, D. T., & Mossakowski, K. N. (2012). Limited English proficiency and psychological distress among Latinos and Asian Americans. *Social Science & Medicine, 75*(6), 1006–1014.

Zhao, X., & Biernat, M. (2017). "Welcome to the US" but "change your name"? Adopting Anglo names and discrimination. *Journal of Experimental Social Psychology, 70*, 59–68.

Zou, L. X., & Cheryan, S. (2017). Two axes of subordination: A new model of racial position. *Journal of Personality and Social Psychology, 112*(5), 696–717.

Acknowledgements

This work was supported by the National Science Foundation SBE Postdoctoral Research Fellowship under Grant No. 2004269 awarded to A. Albuja, the Social Sciences and Humanities Research Council of Canada Postdoctoral Fellowship (Ref: 756–2020-0626) awarded to A. West, and the NSF CAREER Grant BCS-2042433 awarded to S. Gaither.

Cambridge Elements ≡

Applied Social Psychology

Susan Clayton

College of Wooster, Ohio

Susan Clayton is a social psychologist at the College of Wooster in Wooster, Ohio. Her research focuses on the human relationship with nature, how it is socially constructed, and how it can be utilized to promote environmental concern.

About the Series

Many social psychologists have used their research to understand and address pressing social issues, from poverty and prejudice to work and health. Each Element in this series reviews a particular area of applied social psychology. Elements will also discuss applications of the research findings and describe directions for future study.

Cambridge Elements ⁼

Applied Social Psychology

Elements in the Series

Empathy and Concern with Negative Evaluation in Intergroup Relations: Implications for Designing Effective Interventions
Jacquie D. Vorauer

The Psychology of Climate Change Adaptation
Anne van Valkengoed and Linda Steg

Undoing the Gender Binary
Charlotte Chucky Tate, Ella Ben Hagai, and Faye J. Crosby

Selves as Solutions to Social Inequalities: Why Engaging the Full Complexity of Social Identities is Critical to Addressing Disparities
Tiffany N. Brannon, Peter H. Fisher, and Abigail J. Greydanus

Identity Development During STEM Integration for Underrepresented Minority Students
Sophie L. Kuchynka, Alexander E. Gates, and Luis M. Rivera

The Psychology of Effective Activism
Robyn Gulliver, Susilo Wibisono, Kelly S. Fielding, and Winnifred R. Louis

Learning from Video Games (and Everything Else): The General Learning Model
Douglas A. Gentile and J. Ronald Gentile

Climate Change and Human Behavior: Impacts of a Rapidly Changing Climate on Human Aggression and Violence
Andreas Miles-Novelo and Craig A. Anderson

Behavioral Insights for Public Policy: Contextualizing Our Science
Crystal C. Hall and Ines Jurcevic

Entrapment, Escape, and Elevation from Relationship Violence
Wind Goodfriend and Pamela Lassiter Simcock

Two or More: A Comparative Analysis of Multiracial and Multicultural Research
Analia F. Albuja, Alexandria West, and Sarah E. Gaither

A full series listing is available at: www.cambridge.org/EASP

Printed in the United States
by Baker & Taylor Publisher Services